PERFORMANCE
DRIVEN
PARTNERSHIPS

THE MENTAL CONDITIONING
— PLAYBOOK FOR —
MARRIAGE, LEADERSHIP AND LEGACY

MICHELLE A. McELROY

PERFORMANCE-DRIVEN PARTNERSHIP
The Mental Conditioning Playbook for Marriage, Leadership, and Legacy

Michelle A. McElroy
www.aimarriages.com
michelle@aimarriages.com

ISBN 978-1-943343-22-5

Printed in the USA.
All rights reserved

Published by: Destined To Publish | Flossmoor, Illinois
www.DestinedToPublish.com

Dedication

This book is dedicated to the people, the process, and the purpose that shaped me.

x o x o

To my mother, Annie,
Thank you for the strength and resilience you modeled through every season of womanhood and motherhood. Your perseverance taught me how to stand when life demanded more than comfort, and how to keep going when the path wasn't easy. Your life was my first lesson in endurance.

x o x o

To my father, Sam Henderson,
Thank you for showing me what a good man looks like—not just in words, but in action. Because of you, I knew what to look for in a husband, how I deserved to be treated, and what integrity sounds like when it speaks. Your encouragement—decade after decade—reminded me that I could achieve anything I committed my heart to. I carried your belief with me every step of the way.

x o x o

To my children— Miray, Jamari, Janae, and Ramiah,
You are my cheering section, my motivation, and my loudest hype crowd. Everything I build is with you in mind. Watching you believe in me has fueled my purpose more than you'll ever know.

And finally, to my husband, Ray
The best husband on the planet.
My partner.
The love of my life.
The king of my castle.

x o x o

You modeled drive and discipline, and you have given me an unshakable confidence in both who I am and who God created me to be. Thank you for supporting me holistically in every way imaginable. For lifting me high, standing beside me faithfully, and believing in my purpose even when the path was still unfolding. This journey—and this book—would not exist without you.

You are my anchor, my rock, my leader.

Acknowledgments

To my mentor, Dr. Doug McKinley,
Thank you for helping me unravel the journey and recognize the footprints God had already laid before me. Your guidance helped me discover and trust my calling as a counselor, leadership coach, and business owner. You didn't just help me grow professionally—you helped me see myself clearly and supported me every step of the way.

To my writing coach, Neesha Stringfellow,

Thank you for your input, advice, and support. You pushed me to the finish line, and words cannot express my gratitude. You were what I needed and so much more. I'm an author because of you.

To my publisher, Marilyn Alexander,

Thank you for accepting me as a client with no idea what I was doing and an impossible deadline. I appreciate your willingness to work with me and push my project forward to completion with faith and fortitude.

To my family, friends, and clients
Thank you for allowing me to learn from your journeys—both the victories and the lessons—often vicariously. Your stories expanded my compassion, sharpened my wisdom, and deepened my understanding of love, leadership, and life.

To Jesus, my Lord and Savior,

I thank you for every difficult, challenging, painful, joyful, and seemingly impossible life experience. Thank you for stretching me beyond what I thought I was capable of and pushing me closer to who you created me to be. You taught and trained me. You helped me to grow mentally and emotionally. You gave me the opportunity to become more aware, more grounded, and more equipped to help others. You gave me potential and purpose. I am deeply appreciative and grateful for it all.

Contents

Book Dedication

iii

Acknowledgments

v

CHAPTER 1

Draft Day—Understanding the Purpose Behind Your Partnership

1

CHAPTER 2

Behind the Stats—The Real Me Beneath the Title

7

CHAPTER 3

Who Are You? —The Film Study of Self

17

CHAPTER 4

Who Are We? — Team Chemistry and Collective Purpose

51

CHAPTER 5

Game-Time Focus—Playing the Long Game in Life and Love

74

CHAPTER 6

Practice Makes Partnership—Building Championship Habits

92

CHAPTER 7

Building Your Team—The Power of a Purposeful Circle

106

CHAPTER 8

The ROI of Relationship—Why This Book Matters for the Pro Athlete and Spouse

126

CHAPTER 9

The Mission of Us—Crafting Your Marriage Playbook

135

Resource Page

148

CHAPTER 1

Draft Day—Understanding the Purpose Behind Your Partnership

There comes a moment in every marriage—whether you're an everyday couple or a household with stadium lights attached—when you stop and ask yourself, *"Why did God bring us together?"*

Not *how* you met.
Not *when* you got married.
But *why*.

When I began working with couples—especially professional athletes and high-capacity leaders—I realized something quickly: most people know how to fall in love, but very few know how to build a marriage with *purpose*.
A marriage with a *mission*.
A marriage that's strong enough to withstand pressure, transition, success, setbacks, scrutiny, and the emotional demands that come with visibility.

And if you're reading this book, chances are you're ready to make a shift—from accidental to intentional, from surviving to strategizing, from doing marriage on default to leading it with purpose.

This book is about that shift.

But before I teach you the tools, the systems, and the emotional-intelligence frameworks athletes and their spouses need, I must tell you where this mission started for me. Because this assignment—this work—didn't begin when I became a coach. It began long before I realized what God was preparing me for.

Pre-Season Preparation: Where My Mission Truly Began

If you had told me back at Eastern Illinois University—when Ray was grinding through two-a-days and I was working on my master's degree—that someday we'd be helping highly visible couples define the purpose of their marriage, I would've looked at you like you were speaking a foreign language.

To be honest, I wasn't sure of anything back then.

I wasn't sure Ray would make it to the NFL.
I wasn't sure how my purpose would unfold.
I wasn't sure anyone would ever listen to the voice God placed inside of me.
I wasn't sure how two kids from completely different upbringings would grow into the kind of couple that could one day teach others.

But here's the thing:
I wasn't sure about the path, but I was sure about my purpose.

Even then, while I was sitting in lecture halls studying human behavior, communication patterns, and the complexities of emotional development, something in me knew I was designed to help people love better. To help them heal. To help them build relationships rooted in intention, not instability.

And while Ray ran drills on the field—fighting for a future none of us could predict—God was shaping him into a man who would one day speak into the hearts of husbands, fathers, and leaders navigating the pressures of visibility and performance.

We didn't know it at the time, but both of us were in training—not just academically or athletically, but spiritually.

We were being prepared for an assignment that wouldn't make sense until years later.

Back then, our love was young and our dreams were loud. We had no idea that God was weaving two very different stories together for a shared mission—one that would ultimately call us to help couples who live in the spotlight cultivate marriages strong enough to withstand both the pressure and the praise.

Here's what I finally understand:

The same intentionality it takes for an athlete to get drafted, stay in the league, and transition well when the cheering stops... is the exact same intentionality required to build a marriage that will not fold under pressure.

Because talent alone won't sustain a career. And love alone won't sustain a marriage.

Over more than 30 years of marriage—through seasons of elevation, heartbreak, transitions, raising four children, the demands of visibility, and our own personal evolution—I've realized something deeply:

This book had to be written because purpose without tools is pressure. And marriages—especially in high-pressure environments—need both purpose and tools.

We were never just building a life together; God was preparing us to build purpose-filled marriages for others.

And now, I can see it clearly: every course I studied, every practice Ray endured, every moment we fought to stay aligned through seasons of uncertainty... was shaping us for this.

Scouting the Field: Why This Playbook Had to Be Written

There is another reason this book exists—one I cannot ignore.

> **Professional athletes face divorce rates estimated between 60% and 80%—far higher than the national average.**

The pressure of performance, constant transitions, public scrutiny, financial shifts, long-distance seasons, and identity changes create stressors that most couples never have to navigate.

Here's what I wholeheartedly believe:

If athletes develop emotional-intelligence (EQ) skills while they're playing—not after retirement—they can build marriages strong enough to withstand both their career and the inevitable separation of player and team that comes later.

This belief isn't just personal; it's validated by people who know this world intimately.

Former NFL Players Association Executive Director Gene Upshaw once said, "A player's emotional intelligence determines how well he plays the game and how well he lives his life."

And he was right.

EQ isn't soft.
EQ isn't optional.
EQ isn't extra.

It is the difference between staying connected and silently unraveling.
Between leading your home and losing your marriage while winning in your career.
Between being celebrated publicly and suffering privately.

This book exists because couples in high-pressure environments deserve tools—not just prayers, not just hope, not just grit. Tools.

Locker Room Essentials: The Non-Negotiables You Must Carry Into This Journey

Before we go deeper, there are three truths you need to keep close:

1. Your marriage has a divine purpose.

God didn't bring you together accidentally.
Your partnership has an assignment.

2. High-performance marriages are built, not born.

Just like elite athletes, strong marriages require habits, systems, emotional intelligence, and accountability.

3. You can rewrite your relationship story at any time.

Your past doesn't disqualify you.
Your patterns don't define you.
Your mistakes don't imprison you.

The Season Ahead: What You Can Expect as We Build This Team

In the chapters ahead, we're going to walk through:

- Your individual identity and your collective mission
- The creation of your Marriage Mission Statement
- The emotional patterns that shape your communication
- Systems that support connection
- Strategies for handling pressure as a unified team

This book will challenge you.
It will comfort you.
It will sharpen you.
But most importantly, it will equip you.

Your marriage doesn't just have potential—*it has purpose.*

And together, we're about to *activate* it.

CHAPTER 2

Behind the Stats—The Real Me Beneath the Title

People often introduce us with titles—NFL player, wife, husband, mother, father, relationship coach, corporate speaker, counselor, pastor, first lady, mentor, podcast host. And while all of that is true, none of it fully captures who we are at our core.

The truth is, I am a woman who has lived through the highs and lows of life with a professional athlete. I am the wife of a six-year veteran NFL player and let me tell you—the platform never departs, whether your spouse is a current or retired player. That's one of the beautiful and complicated things about being married to an athlete: *the spotlight stays even when the salary does not.* For many NFL families, that platform becomes both a blessing and a burden.

Reframed Narrative: Finding (and Losing) Ourselves in the NFL

When Ray was actively playing, life felt amazing—almost surreal. It wasn't just that things were good; it felt like we were good because everything around us looked good. We were young, in love, and living out a dream most people only imagine. For a while, we weren't battling the struggles our peers were facing. We weren't job hunting. We weren't drowning in student loans. We weren't counting pennies or questioning our next move.

Instead, we were relocating with ease, setting up a beautiful home, buying a brand-new SUV, and planning the wedding and honeymoon of our dreams—*instantly*. It felt like reward season. Promise fulfilled. Purpose confirmed. And I had a front row seat to every celebratory moment.

Family and friends celebrated alongside us, watching Ray's hard-earned journey reach the mountaintop. We bought tickets year after year so they could share in the joy, the pride, the glory. And honestly? We loved it. Who wouldn't?

We spent four whole years floating in this unbelievable feeling of success—success that whispered, "*You made it. You belong here. This is who you are now.*"

But then year five hit.
And everything we attached our identity to got tested.

Ray's contract ended, and the Colts chose not to renew it. Weeks passed. Then months. Silence. No callbacks. No workouts. No interest.

And suddenly, the life that once felt like proof of our worth started to feel like it was slipping through our fingers.

Then Carolina called—a breath of hope. A second chance. A familiar face on the team. A warm-weather city. A new jersey. A new opportunity to rebuild the story. "*This is it,*" we thought. "*Our next chapter.*"

But it wasn't.
Cut by the Panthers.

Again, dream deferred.
Again, our identity shaken.

Ray sat out an entire year. And let me tell you, a year on the sideline feels like a lifetime when your entire adult identity has been wrapped in a uniform you're no longer wearing.

Then, by what we can only call a miracle, Ray received an offer to join our home team, the Chicago Bears. Hope returned. Purpose felt restored. We felt *seen* again.

But even that season was short-lived.
After one year with the Bears, he was picked up... released...
then picked back up by the Detroit Lions for the final four games of the season.

A whirlwind.
A scramble.
A cycle of hope and heartbreak.

And somewhere in all of that movement—every contract, every cut, every transition—we realized something we didn't understand in the beginning:

We had accidentally placed our identity in the NFL—not in God, not in purpose, and not in who we were created to be outside of the game.

The highs felt like confirmation that we mattered.
The lows felt like personal failure.
And the uncertainty felt like our entire future was on trial.

That's what happens when *where you play* becomes *who you believe you are.*

And that... is where the real work began.

People see the NFL title and assume a lifetime of luxury follows every player home.

But here's the truth no one tells you:

The money may leave, but the expectations don't.
The fame may fade, but the pressure remains.
The title may expire, but the platform stays attached
to your name forever.

The Reality No One Prepares You For

During their playing years, the league encourages players to focus solely on football. And on paper, that makes sense—football is their career, their commitment, their contribution to a team depending on them.

But here's where it becomes complicated:

From ages 8 to 22, most athletes spend over a decade training for a dream only 3% will achieve. And even for those who make it, the *average NFL career is just 3.3 years.* Meanwhile, the average person will work for 40 to 50 years.

Do the math: that leaves 37–47 years of unclaimed identity, unfulfilled purpose, and unanswered questions.

After six seasons, football was done with Ray.
And like many players, he was hoping for at least ten.

When he got released, he wasn't ready emotionally, financially, or personally. We tried to pivot by investing in a business during his final season, hoping to create stability. But the business failed, and our partner began using company funds for personal reasons.

Football was over.
Our business collapsed.
Ray spiraled into depression.

And I was home with a newborn, a four-year-old, and a two-year-old—trying to stretch one income that didn't match three growing children.

People still assumed we were "set for life," because that's the narrative the world sells:
"*He played in the NFL—he must be rich.*"

But here's the truth:
Entry-level jobs in the real world paid less than
our cost of childcare.
We had more expectations on our shoulders than
resources in our hands.
And the emotional load of public perception
weighed on Ray heavily.

Everyone still expected him to perform, provide, appear strong, and stay grateful—even as he silently battled disappointment, *identity loss*, guilt, and shame.

This is the part of the story few ever hear.

Because when an athlete transitions out of the league, the cheering stops—but the expectations don't.
The cameras go away, but the pressure intensifies.
The income slows down, but the opinions multiply.
Family asks for help.
Friends assume you're still wealthy.
Strangers expect generosity.

And meanwhile, the man you love is standing there trying to process his own grief while carrying the disappointments of everyone else.

Our Post-Game Reality Check

The two years after Ray retired were the defining years of our marriage—and of who I was becoming as a wife, as a woman, and as a purpose-driven partner.

For two years:
we argued,
I fussed,
we cried,
I prayed,
we struggled financially,
and we endured an emotional cycle that felt never-ending.

We were living on survival mode—emotionally, spiritually, financially.

And looking back, those two years were not just about
money or transition.
They were about identity. Purpose. Expectations. Pressure.
Loss. And rediscovery.

This is where emotional intelligence entered my life, even before I had the language for it.

The Turning Point: Emotional Intelligence in Real Time

Our game-changing moment arrived when a friend handed me a book: *The Power of a Praying Wife.*

It didn't teach me *that* I needed to pray.
It taught me how to pray, and what to pray for.

Day by day, something *undeniable* began to shift in me. God was reshaping me in ways I could no longer deny. What started subtly became certain: I was being transformed from the inside out. The internal shift became my turning point—subtle at first, then absolute, like a momentum swing mid-game. It was like recalibrating my emotional muscle memory one rep at a time. God was rewriting me in real time.

- I became emotionally aware of Ray's perspective.
- I began to see the pain beneath his silence.
- I learned to pause before reacting and listen before assuming.
- I shifted from disappointment to destiny.
- I focused less on the losses and more on God's future for us.
- I realized my words could either suffocate his spirit or speak life into his purpose.

This was my very first encounter with emotional intelligence—self-awareness, empathy, self-management, and relational discernment.
Not in a classroom.
Not in a workshop.
But right in the middle of my own living room.

From the Sidelines to Significance

At Eastern Illinois University , Ray loved communication classes— he had no idea those seeds would blossom into a global purpose.

While with the Colts, he took every opportunity offered to speak in schools and churches. Post-NFL, he accepted a national speaking role with Sportsworld, traveling across the country to tell young people about the greatest decision he ever made accepting Christ as his Savior.

That assignment shifted everything.

No, our lives didn't suddenly become perfect.
But we were aligned.
We were moving forward.
We were operating in purpose—even when circumstances
didn't match it yet.

Meanwhile, I was developing lesson plans at church, nurturing youth, studying biblical frameworks, and deepening my understanding of developmental psychology. Ray eventually connected with the Chicago Bears' chaplain and was invited to lead multiple team chapels.

Before long, we were ministering together—five weekly services over five years. Ray led chapel, coaches' study, and players' study, I led the wives' study, and we both led couples' study.

Destiny fulfilled.

Not overnight.
Not easily.
Not without tears.
But fulfilled.

Who Am I Now?

I didn't come up in church culture—I came up in *dependence on God.* My faith wasn't formed in pews; it was built in pressure. It was shaped through long nights, unanswered questions, tear-stained prayers, and a deep belief that God would meet me in the middle of my struggle. At the time, I didn't realize I was in training. I thought I was just trying to survive.

What I couldn't see then was that God was conditioning me for a greater assignment. He was developing endurance in me before responsibility. He was strengthening my spiritual core long before I stepped into marriage, leadership, and environments marked by extreme highs and crushing lows. Season after season, my faith was tested—stretched, challenged, and refined—until it became resilient enough to withstand pressure without breaking.

Looking back now, I see it clearly: God wasn't just walking me through hardship. He was preparing a woman He could trust— one who could stand steady when circumstances shifted and still believe Him in the process. He was preparing me to be the wife of a professional athlete.

The highs and lows of life as an athlete's wife shaped me into a Spirit-filled woman of faith—not because of tradition, but because of transformation.

My faith was built in the fire.
My purpose was shaped in adversity.
My emotional intelligence matured through lived experience.
And my voice emerged through obedience and expectancy.

God's faith in me—His divine provision, His relentless assignment— has willed me into the version of Michelle I am today... and the version I am continually becoming.

Are You the Wife of an Athlete?

Then this book is for you too.

If you're a woman navigating the spotlight, the pressure, the expectations, the uncertainty, the transitions, the emotional load no one prepares you for—you are not alone.

I wrote this book with you in mind.

Your marriage has purpose.

Your partnership has power.

And your healing, your confidence, and your emotional intelligence matter.

This is your permission to exhale.

To be honest about your journey.

To see yourself.

To understand him.

To prepare for the future God has already designed for you both.

CHAPTER 3

Who Are You? — The Film Study of Self

Every person is born with a unique design—a blend of personality, temperament, strengths, and purpose that makes you who you are. That design influences how you love, how you lead, how you communicate, and how you show up in relationships.

> **Every elite performer knows this truth: before you can master the game, you have to master yourself.**

Your identity—the real you behind the highlight reels, successes, failures, or expectations—is the foundation of everything you build.

Titles change.
Positions shift.
Careers evolve.
But your identity is the one thing you carry into every
season of your life.

So let me ask you the same question I ask the couples I coach:
Who are you outside of the title, the contract, the career, or the jersey? Who are you when no one is cheering, no one is demanding, and no one needs anything from you?

Are you a son, a daughter, a partner, a leader,
a teammate, a friend?
And more importantly—*what drives you? What centers you? What shapes how you love and how you show up?*

When you understand who you are *at the core*, you gain clarity, confidence, and purpose. You stop living on autopilot and start operating with intention—not just in your marriage, but in every arena of your life. Understanding your identity isn't just a spiritual concept—it's the foundation for emotional intelligence, relational health, and purpose-driven decision-making. When you know who you really are, you stop reacting to life and start leading your life.

This is your invitation to discover that version of you.

The First Season Under Pressure

I remember Ray's first season with the Indianapolis Colts like it was yesterday. He was deep in the grind—meetings, practices, film study, rookie expectations—and I was in the final stretch of my own season: graduate school. Our rhythm was built around his schedule. I'd catch him on home-game weekends, maybe an off-day here or there, and during the bye week if our schedules aligned. We were two people in love, running our own races, hoping our finish lines would eventually merge.

When the season wrapped and I walked across the stage with my master's degree, I packed my car like an undrafted free agent heading into camp—everything I owned stuffed into a trunk and backseat—and I drove to Indianapolis to start my life with the man I believed God had chosen for me. One month of living together and we decided to get married at the justice of the peace. Quick decision. Big leap. Full heart.

For a few months, it felt like we were winning—like marriage was our undefeated streak. We were in marital bliss, convinced that love, faith, and intentionality were enough to carry us through any challenge. After all, that's what young couples believe: "If we love each other enough, the rest will work itself out."

But then the real season started.

Living together full-time exposed things we didn't even know were in our playbooks. Our differences weren't small flags—they were full-blown reviewable plays under the stadium lights. The unseen began surfacing old wounds, childhood patterns, unspoken fears, and deeply rooted insecurities that had never been stretched, tested, or conditioned.

No one told us that marriage was where your spouse would inadvertently run routes straight through your unhealed places.
No one told us that the person you love most would also trigger the parts of you you've avoided the longest.
No one told us that our default settings—formed long before we met—would show up like unscouted weaknesses on game day.

We thought we knew each other.
We thought we knew ourselves.
But we were rookies—talented, hopeful, and unprepared for the real demands of partnership.

Marriage is its own league.
And just like the NFL, it exposes exactly who
you are under pressure.
Not to shame you, but to shape you.

Not to break you, but to build you.
Not to condemn you, but to call you higher.

Those early years taught us a hard truth:

> **Love might draft you into marriage, but identity determines whether you can stay in the league.**

And neither of us knew our identity yet.

Under the Helmet: When the Game Reveals the Man-

Ray's Perspective

They say pressure doesn't create character—it reveals it. And nowhere is that truer than in the life of a professional athlete.

Answering the question "*Who are you?*" forced me to confront a hard reality: many of us live with two identities.

There's the perceived identity—who we think we are.
And then there's the true identity—who we actually are when the lights are off.

Before marrying Michelle, I believed I knew exactly who I was. I saw myself as strong, confident, accomplished, respectable. Those traits weren't lies—but they weren't the whole truth either. Much of what I projected was shaped by the expectations placed on me as a professional athlete. *The league, the locker room, the media, and even fans all expect you to be unshakable.* Tough. Always in control. Always winning—on and off the field.

You perform.

You suit up emotionally the same way you do physically—helmet on, chin strap tight, vulnerabilities tucked away. You compartmentalize fear. You bury doubt. You ignore emotional injuries the same way you're taught to play through physical pain. Because in this world, weakness feels like it costs you reps, respect, and opportunity.

But the truth is—we're not superhuman. We're human under pressure.

And what we don't deal with in private eventually shows up in the most intimate spaces of our lives—our marriages, our homes, our closest relationships.

I carried scars I never addressed. Doubts I never named. Fears I never processed. And I brought all of that into marriage without realizing it. It wasn't until I was forced to honestly answer the question "Who are you—really?" that true growth began.

Marriage didn't expose me to shame me.
It exposed me to shape me.

That's when I learned that real strength isn't about how hard you hit—it's about how honestly you face yourself. And real intimacy doesn't happen through performance; it happens through truth.

I've come to deeply appreciate my wife for pushing us—sometimes uncomfortably—to wrestle with this question. Because if you want a partnership that performs at an elite level, you have to be willing to do elite inner work.

You can't build championship chemistry while hiding behind a jersey.

And you can't lead a marriage well if you've never learned how to lead yourself.

The Mental Load

Professional athletes enter adulthood at full speed. Whether you're fresh out of college, newly drafted, undrafted but determined, or already a few seasons in, the truth is the same: you're young, highly visible, and expected to perform at a level most people never experience—on or off the field. Some of you brought your high school or college sweetheart along for the ride. Others married early into your career. And some are navigating the complexity of dating while trying to establish yourself professionally. No matter your relationship status, identity becomes the quiet battle beneath the loud expectations.

From the moment you step into training camp, you meet every personality imaginable—the jokester, the loudmouth, the party guy, the introvert, the Bible-believer, the overly serious one, the natural leader, the passive follower, and the player determined to lose himself before he truly finds himself. Whether you're a rookie fighting for a roster spot, a veteran trying to hold your ground, or a transitioning athlete figuring out life beyond the game, you notice something: you're all living similar dreams but carrying very different stories.

And somewhere in those locker rooms, team hotels, and practice fields, it hits you...
Every one of you is trying to figure out who you are—beyond the jersey, beyond the contract, beyond the accolades.

As a relationship coach and wife of a professional athlete, I know this the truth:

> **Even while you're "on top of the world," adulthood in a high-pressure, high-visibility profession exposes your core.**

It reveals your insecurities, your unhealed childhood wounds, your relational patterns, and your blind spots—often faster than you're ready for.

It doesn't matter whether you're in year one or year ten, active or retired, engaged or newly married, a powerhouse couple or navigating two careers at once—*the journey requires more than talent. It demands emotional maturity, identity clarity, and self-awareness.*

Why? Because:

Pressure amplifies whatever is already inside you.

Money magnifies what you haven't healed.

Visibility exposes what you've been avoiding.

Relationships reveal who you truly are when the crowds are gone.

This is why it's not enough to train your body
and mind for the game.
You must train your inner life for the journey.

Knowing who you are at your core—your values, your wounds, your tendencies, your emotional patterns—becomes the anchor that sustains you when the applause fades, when injuries hit, when transitions come, when fans move on, when roles shift at home, and when life demands more from you than performance.

Because no matter your demographic—rookie, veteran, retired athlete, or power couple—*identity is your foundation.* And when you're secure in who you are, everything else—your marriage, your purpose, your career, your leadership—strengthens from the inside out.

Developing Your First Teammate: You

In sports, success starts long before game day. It begins in the weight room, in film study, in discipline behind the scenes. The same is true in marriage. The best way to be a strong teammate in your relationship is to first become a disciplined partner to yourself.

We often talk about partnerships as something shared with another person—but what about the one you build within?

> **Before you can lead, love, or lift someone else, you must learn how to lead yourself.**

You can't pour into a spouse, team, or family if your own emotional tank is empty.

Building a purposeful partnership with yourself means putting in reps—mental, emotional, and spiritual. It's knowing your triggers, your tendencies, your recovery strategies. It's watching your own film and learning how you respond under pressure. That's where real growth happens.

There's a playbook for this work—it's called the *mental conditioning framework*.

Mental Conditioning Framework™ (MCF)

A framework for emotional development, relational resilience, and purpose-driven leadership during and beyond peak performance seasons.

Mental conditioning is the intentional practice of developing emotional awareness, disciplined self-leadership, relational clarity, and purposeful influence so individuals and couples can perform well under pressure, transition successfully through life seasons, and build legacy beyond their title, role, or career.

Unlike traditional mental toughness—which focuses primarily on endurance and grit—mental conditioning develops the *inner systems* that sustain long-term success: identity, emotional regulation, relational intelligence, and leadership capacity. It prepares individuals not just to compete, but to live well, love well, and lead well—both during high-performance years and after the spotlight fades.

At its core, mental conditioning equips people to move from reaction to regulation, from performance to purpose, and from individual success to collective impact.

The Four Pillars of Mental Conditioning

1. Self-Examination

Awareness before adjustment.

Self-examination is the disciplined practice of observing oneself honestly—thoughts, emotions, triggers, habits, and patterns—without judgment or denial. It is the "film study" of your inner life.

This pillar develops:

- Identity clarity beyond titles and roles
- Awareness of emotional triggers and behavioral defaults
- Understanding of how past experiences shape present reactions
- Reflective practices that reveal habits and responses needing realignment

Self-examination answers the foundational question: "Who am I, really—and why do I respond the way I do under pressure?"

Without self-examination, growth is accidental. With it, growth becomes intentional.

2. Self-Governance

Leadership over self before leadership over others.

Self-governance is the ability to regulate emotions, manage impulses, and make intentional choices aligned with values rather than circumstances. It is where awareness turns into discipline.

This pillar develops:

- Character identity—current and desired
- Emotional regulation under stress
- Decision-making rooted in purpose, not ego or fear
- The capacity to pause, reflect, and respond wisely
- Tracking for developmental and performance progress

Self-governance answers the question: "Now that I see myself clearly, how will I choose to lead myself differently?"

This is the difference between being controlled by pressure and being strengthened by it.

3. Relational Consciousness

Seeing beyond self to understand impact.

Relational consciousness is the awareness of how one's emotions, communication style, and behaviors affect others—especially intimate partners, teammates, family members, and colleagues.

This pillar develops:

- Empathy and perspective-taking
- Awareness of relational dynamics and power imbalances
- The ability to navigate conflict without damaging connection
- Purpose-driven insight that leads to intentional execution

Relational consciousness answers the question: "How do my internal choices shape the health of the relationships I'm part of?"

This is where personal development becomes relational maturity.

4. Relational Leadership

Using influence to build, not dominate.

Relational leadership is the intentional use of influence to create emotional safety, alignment, growth, and purpose within relationships and communities. It is leadership expressed through service, responsibility, and example—not control.

This pillar develops:

- Shared vision and collective purpose
- The ability to lead partnerships, families, and teams with integrity
- The capacity to mentor, model, and multiply healthy behaviors
- Strategic growth with measurable impact

Relational leadership answers the question: "How do I steward my influence to elevate others and build something that lasts?"

This is where personal transformation becomes legacy.

> **Mental conditioning is not about fixing what's broken—it's about strengthening what must last.**

It trains individuals to:

- Know themselves (self-examination)
- Lead themselves (self-governance)
- Understand others (relational consciousness)
- Build with purpose (relational leadership)

And when applied within marriage, it transforms love into mission, partnership into legacy, and success into something that truly endures.

Let's focus on the first two: *self-examination and self-governance.* These are your off-season drills—the unseen work that determines how you show up when life's game gets tough. The more you study *you,* the more equipped you are to perform with wisdom, patience, and grace—on and off the field.

Monitoring Your Inner Coach

When I was young, I spent a lot of time alone.

I grew up in a single-parent household with my mother and my older sister during my most formative years. My mother was a phenomenal provider—she kept food on the table and a roof over our heads—but she didn't have the emotional tools to teach us how to build healthy relationships. Parenting wasn't modeled through connection, communication, or emotional regulation. It was modeled through survival.

My sister is four years older than me, and we didn't have a close relationship. There wasn't a lot of warmth, teamwork, or emotional safety in our home. What I learned early—without anyone ever saying it out loud—was that relationships were something you endured, not something you trained for.

I adapted.

In friendships, I learned two plays and ran them repeatedly:

- I stayed silent and people-pleased, hoping not to lose the relationship
- I cut people off completely when I felt hurt, misunderstood, or rejected

That was my relational playbook: shut down or shut off.

At the time, it felt like self-protection. And honestly, it worked—for a while. Those strategies helped me survive my childhood and young adulthood. But survival skills don't automatically translate into *marriage skills*.

I didn't realize that until I got married.

When Ray and I started building a life together, I unknowingly brought those same habits into our home. I didn't know how damaging they would become once we were no longer dating but living, parenting, and doing life together every single day. I didn't yet understand that just because a strategy got you through one season doesn't mean it's qualified to take you into the next.

I also didn't understand that you can rewire yourself.
I thought, *this is just who I am.*
And for a long time, who I was had been enough to get me by.

But marriage has a way of exposing what survival keeps hidden.

The Moment I Changed the Game

One day, after Ray left for work, I put the kids down for a nap. The house was quiet. No distractions. No noise. No audience.

I lay prostrate on the living room floor and prayed one of the most honest prayers of my life:

"God, fix me."

Not fix Ray.
Not fix our circumstances.
Not fix our season.

Fix *me*.

That was my surrender moment. I let go of my ego, my need to be right, and the armor I had built around my insecurities. I released the false narratives I had carried for years—feelings of inadequacy, rejection, and the belief that withdrawing was strength.

And that's when something shifted—not slowly, not vaguely, but decisively.

I began to observe my marriage differently.

I started studying my interactions with Ray the way an athlete studies an opponent—paying attention to patterns, tendencies, triggers, and tells. But even more importantly, I started studying *myself*.

I asked questions I had never asked before:

- Why does this comment trigger me?
- Why do I shut down instead of speaking up?
- Why do I feel the need to protect myself when there's no real threat?

This was my first real experience with intentional self-examination.

I was developing my inner coach.

Training the Voice That Trains You

Every athlete knows the power of coaching. But what many don't realize is that...

> **... the most influential coach you'll ever have is the one inside your own head.**

Your inner coach shapes how you:

- Interpret conflict
- Recover from mistakes
- Communicate under pressure
- Respond when you feel unseen or misunderstood

For years, my inner coach was harsh, reactive, and rooted in old wounds. It didn't correct—it criticized. It didn't encourage—it protected at all costs.

Through prayer, reflection, and emotional awareness, I began retraining that voice.

Instead of reacting automatically, I learned to pause.
Instead of withdrawing, I learned to engage.
Instead of defending myself, I learned to understand myself.

That's *self-examination* in action.

I didn't just become more aware of Ray through observation—I became more aware of *me*. And once I learned how to coach myself with clarity, compassion, and accountability, everything about how

I showed up in my marriage began to change. Because when you upgrade your inner coach, you change how you play the game.

Every athlete knows the power of a good coach—but what about the one inside your head? That inner voice shapes your confidence, focus, and resilience. Some of us have a positive inner coach—encouraging, steady, faith-filled. Others have an inner critic—harsh, demanding, and impossible to please.

If your self-talk is negative, fear-based, or rooted in past trauma, it will affect every area of your game—your work, your marriage, your parenting, and your peace. The words you speak to yourself become the strategy you live by.

So ask yourself: *What kind of coach are you to yourself?*

Do you speak life into your potential, or do you tear yourself down after every mistake?

God calls us to renew our minds (Romans 12:2)—to retrain our thought patterns the same way an athlete retrains muscle memory.

Why This Internal Work Matters—Even Professionally

Before we move on, let's pause and acknowledge *why* this internal work really matters. This isn't just about emotional growth for your marriage—it's about mastering the mindset that affects every part of your life. Because how you handle your emotions doesn't clock out when you leave home or step off the field. It shows up in the locker room, in the boardroom, and in how you respond when life throws a curveball.

Your emotional intelligence is the silent MVP behind your performance—personally, professionally, and spiritually.

Let's be honest—your emotional game impacts everything. The way you think under pressure, communicate with your spouse, resolve conflict, lead others, or bounce back from setbacks—it all starts from within. In sports, we call it *mental toughness*, but true toughness goes deeper than muscle or mindset. It's about staying grounded, emotionally aware, and spiritually aligned when the pressure is on. That's emotional development at work.

And it's not just a "nice-to-have." Research proves it. Studies show that almost 60% of success in leadership and performance comes from emotional development 2—not IQ or skillset.

People who invest in understanding themselves handle stress better, recover faster, and make more balanced decisions when the stakes are high.

In fact, companies that train their teams in emotional development see measurable gains in productivity, communication, and overall morale. The evidence is clear: when your emotions work *for* you instead of against you, you lead and love more effectively.

Think of this inner work as your *mental conditioning program*—not just for your marriage, but for your career and calling. You wouldn't hit the field without warming up or studying film. Likewise, you can't step into your purpose without preparing your inner life. Self-examination and self-governance are your warm-up and playbook for every arena you step into—home, work, locker room, or boardroom.

When you strengthen your mental condition, you're not just becoming a better spouse—you're becoming a stronger leader, teammate, and person of influence. You'll notice that your patience deepens, your communication sharpens, and your discernment grows. You'll stop reacting out of old patterns and start responding from a place of wisdom, faith, and control.

And that right there—that's championship-level living.

A Note for the Wife of a Professional Athlete

You are not just the woman behind the man—you are the steady force beside him.

> **In a world built on constant motion, competition, and scrutiny, you are the grounding presence that keeps the family anchored in love, faith, and focus.**

Your role carries a quiet power—one that doesn't always make the highlight reel but holds the entire team together.

When your husband walks into the arena, he may represent the name on the jersey—but you represent the heart behind it. You create stability in transition, peace in pressure, and perspective amid unpredictability. You are both the calm and the catalyst—a partner who leads with wisdom, emotional intelligence, and unwavering support.

Your value within the marital team isn't measured in statistics or game-day appearances. It's revealed in the way you protect his peace, nurture his purpose, and cover your household in prayer and strategy. Your love becomes his recovery space. Your discernment helps him lead with clarity. Your emotional intelligence sets the tone for your family's environment—one built on grace, growth, and grounded communication.

You are the emotional quarterback of your home—reading the plays, anticipating needs, and adjusting with composure when the unexpected hits. Your ability to regulate emotions, manage tension, and communicate truth in love creates a safe space where vulnerability and strength can coexist. That's the foundation of real partnership—the kind that outlasts seasons and contracts.

Your influence is not secondary—it's synergistic. The way you show up emotionally, spiritually, and mentally affects how your family performs as a unit. You bring balance to the drive. Warmth to the ambition. Faith to the fatigue. You remind your partner that his worth isn't based on performance, but on purpose.

And when you invest in your own self-awareness and emotional growth, you elevate everything connected to you. You become not just a supporter, but a strategist—a partner who leads from within. You embody what it means to be a *Performance Partner*: intentional, intuitive, and anchored in truth.

Because when you're strong, centered, and emotionally healthy, your family wins—every single time.

(Note: Although I'm addressing wives here, this information can apply to any spouse of a professional athlete, regardless of gender.)

The Lifelong Training Program

This inner work isn't a one-time drill; it's a lifelong journey of personal discovery. You're constantly evolving, growing, and adjusting your form. Never stop studying yourself. Never stop improving your spiritual conditioning.

Your relationship with yourself sets the tone for every other relationship in your life. The best gift you can offer your spouse—and your legacy—is a whole, self-aware, emotionally mature version of you.

Now let's get practical. Before we talk about partnership with someone else, let's look at where it all started—with you.

The Locker Room of the Mind

Every great athlete knows the locker room isn't just where you suit up—it's where you *show up*. It's the space where reflection meets preparation. Where you rewind, review, and realign before stepping back onto the field. That's what emotional intelligence offers you—a spiritual locker room for your mind and heart.

Emotional intelligence begins with self-examination: knowing your strengths, recognizing your limitations, understanding your triggers, and being honest about what drives your emotions. It's like walking into the locker room after a tough game and owning your performance—no excuses, no denial, just truth and growth.

Self-examination asks, *"What's really going on inside me?"*

It's the foundation of all personal development, because you can't manage what you don't recognize. In the same way a player studies film to spot weaknesses and improve plays, mental conditioning invites you to study *yourself*—your thoughts, your reactions, your patterns.

Film Study: Reviewing the Plays of Your Inner Life

Before every season and every game, athletes spend hours studying film—analyzing previous games to identify both victories and mistakes. They review how they moved, where they hesitated, and what strategies worked under pressure. That same process can—and should—happen in your spiritual and emotional life.

Film study of your *inner life* means looking back at your childhood, upbringing, and past experiences with curiosity, not condemnation. It's asking:

- What emotional plays do I keep running that no longer serve me?
- How did my family of origin shape how I communicate, love, or protect myself?
- Where do my old habits still dictate how I show up in my marriage or relationships?

When you review those past plays through a lens of grace and growth, you gain insight into the areas God wants to strengthen. Your past doesn't define you—it *informs* you. Every replay, every misstep, every highlight becomes spiritual footage that helps you understand how God has been coaching you all along.

Spiritual Growth: From Film to Formation

The goal is not just to *see* the past—it's to *learn* from it. The more you understand your emotional patterns, the more you can partner with the Holy Spirit to reshape them. This is the sacred process of *renewing your mind* (Romans 12:2).

Film study without practice is pointless.

Mental conditioning becomes spiritual discipline when it moves from awareness to transformation.

- *Self-examination* asks, "*What do I feel and why?*"

- *Self-governance* responds, "*Now that I see it, how will I handle it differently?*"

That's where spiritual growth happens—in the gap between recognition and response.

When you apply that to marriage, especially within the world of professional athletics, you begin to see your relationship as a team sport where both partners are growing, adjusting, and learning the plays of purpose together.

Studying the Film of Your Own Faith and Emotions: A Personal Perspective

As the wife of a professional athlete, you may feel like your days are a constant rotation of games, travel, transitions, and public expectations. But behind the noise, your emotional development becomes your personal playbook.

Your *film study* might look like revisiting how you were raised to handle disappointment, silence, or success. Maybe you learned early on to "stay strong" instead of expressing emotion, or to hold it together no matter what. But mental conditioning invites you to step into the locker room of your inner life and ask, "*Where did I learn that? Is it still serving me—or do I need to rewrite that play?*"

This kind of awareness allows you to love more freely, communicate more clearly, and support your spouse with deeper empathy. You begin to lead from the inside out—grounded, emotionally mature, and spiritually centered.

Your love becomes steady, not reactionary. Your peace becomes contagious. Your presence becomes a form of leadership—because when you know yourself, you no longer lose yourself trying to manage everyone else.

The Character Development Process™

A Performance Framework for Becoming Your Best Self—On and Off the Field

The *Character Development Process™* is a *daily mental conditioning system* designed to help high-capacity individuals—especially athletes and leaders—evaluate, refine, and execute their personal growth with the same discipline they bring to their craft.

At its core, this process asks three foundational questions—the kind every elite performer must confront to elevate their game:

Am I operating at the best version of myself right now?
(Current performance assessment)

Who do I want to become?
(Future development target)

How do I want to be perceived by others—consistently, under pressure, and over time?
(Game film through the lens of impact and influence)

This is not about perfection.
It's about awareness, adjustment, and execution.

Just like physical training requires honest film study, strength assessments, and skill refinement, character development requires intentional self-examination, disciplined self-governance, and consistent reps toward becoming who you're called to be.

Phase 1: Current Roster—Who You Are Right Now

This is your *baseline evaluation.*
No judgment. No ego. Just truth.

Ask yourself:

- What character traits are currently *showing up consistently?*
- Which ones are helping me perform well—in relationships, leadership, and decision-making?

List Your Characteristics Currently Working for You

These are your *starter-level strengths*—the traits already earning playing time.

Phase 2: Draft Board—Who You Want to Become

This phase is about *intentional recruitment.*
You're identifying the qualities you need to develop to compete at the next level of life—not just career.

Ask yourself:

- What traits do elite leaders, spouses, and teammates possess that I need to develop?
- What qualities would elevate my personal and professional game?

List the Characteristics You Desire to Develop

These are your *developmental prospects*—high upside, requiring reps and refinement.

Phase 3: Championship Standard—Your Highest-Level Self

This is your *peak performance profile.*
Who are you when you're locked in, aligned, and executing with purpose?

Ask yourself:

- If I were operating at my highest level, how would I show up consistently?
- How would people experience me when pressure is high and the stakes are real?

List Characteristics of Your Highest-Level Self

This is your *championship character standard*—the version of you built to last.

Daily Execution: Using the Character Development List as Your Personal Scorecard

Once your list is complete, it becomes your *daily performance gauge.*

Not to shame you.
Not to condemn you.
But to coach you.

Each day, ask:

- Did my actions align with the character traits I'm developing?
- Where did I execute well?
- Where do I need to adjust tomorrow?

This process allows for *real-time evaluation without ego, pride, judgment, or self-condemnation,* because you understand one core truth:

You are in training—not on trial.

Just like athletes track reps, recovery, and execution—not just wins and losses—this list helps you track *growth, awareness, and progress* through intentional self-governance.

- It replaces vague self-improvement with clear performance standards
- It transforms personal growth into a trainable system
- It builds consistency through daily reps, not emotional swings
- It keeps you focused on becoming, not pretending

This is how character is built:

- Rep by rep
- Decision by decision

- Season by season

And when character improves, everything else follows—your leadership, your relationships, your marriage, and your legacy.

The Takeaway: You Are Both the Player and the Coach

Self-examination isn't about perfection—it's about perspective.

Every player knows that mistakes don't end the game—they teach you how to win the next one.

Give yourself permission to study your film, analyze your patterns, and ask God for new plays. You are both the player and the coach of your inner life, with the Holy Spirit as your ultimate guide.

When you embrace emotional development as a spiritual discipline, your awareness becomes your strength, your self-control becomes your power, and your peace becomes your victory.

When you master the locker room within—you can handle any arena you step into.

Once you understand who *you* are—your patterns, triggers, and purpose—the next step is learning who *we* are. Your greatest growth will often come through the person God placed beside you.

Self-examination is powerful—but it's incomplete without movement.

In sports, watching film without adjusting your training plan doesn't change outcomes. You can review every play, name every mistake, and still show up on game day running the same routes, reacting the same way, and repeating the same errors. Awareness alone doesn't win championships. Application does.

That's where self-governance begins.

Self-governance is the moment you stop saying, "*This is just who I am,*" and start asking, "*Who do I need to become for the next season of my life?*"

Once you've examined yourself—your emotional patterns, your triggers, your internal dialogue, your default reactions—the responsibility shifts. You now have a choice. And that choice is whether you will continue to play on instinct alone or begin to play with intention.

Self-governance is learning how to *manage yourself under pressure.*

It's choosing not to react just because something feels familiar.
It's slowing your response instead of letting old
patterns call the play.
It's deciding that your emotions will inform you—but they will
no longer control you.

This is the difference between talent and discipline.
Between potential and longevity.
Between surviving seasons and sustaining purpose.

Calling Audibles in Real Time

Self-governance shows up in real moments, not ideal ones.

It's when:

- You feel yourself shutting down—and choose to stay engaged
- You want to lash out—and choose to pause
- You feel misunderstood—and choose clarity over defensiveness
- You feel exposed—and choose honesty over withdrawal

This isn't about perfection. It's about *awareness in motion.*

Every athlete knows that mid-game adjustments matter just as much as preparation. Coaches call audibles. Players adjust assignments. Leaders take responsibility when a play breaks down. In the same way, self-governance allows you to adjust emotionally *while the game is still being played.*

Instead of replaying regret after the moment passes, you begin learning how to course-correct in the moment.

That's maturity.
That's leadership.
That's growth.

Replacing Old Plays with Better Ones

One of the hardest truths about growth is this:
Just because a strategy protected you once doesn't mean it should lead you now.

Many of the emotional habits we bring into marriage were formed in earlier seasons—childhood, adolescence, survival years. They helped us cope. They helped us endure. But marriage doesn't require coping—it requires partnership.

Self-governance is the discipline of replacing outdated emotional plays with healthier ones.

- Silence becomes communication

- Control becomes collaboration

- Withdrawal becomes vulnerability

- Reactivity becomes regulation

You don't erase your past—you retrain your responses.

This is where emotional development becomes practical. You stop labeling yourself and start coaching yourself. You recognize your tendencies without excusing them. You take ownership not just of what you feel, but of how you act.

And when one partner begins to govern themselves with clarity and consistency, it changes the entire dynamic of the relationship.

Self-Governance Changes Everything

Self-governance doesn't just strengthen marriages—it strengthens leaders.

Athletes who learn to regulate emotions handle pressure better. Spouses who learn to respond instead of
react create safer homes.
Couples who practice self-governance reduce unnecessary conflict and increase trust.

This is how private growth produces public stability.

When you govern yourself well:

- Your communication improves
- Your confidence deepens
- Your relationships stabilize
- Your purpose sharpens

You stop being ruled by old narratives and start leading from intention.

And that's the point where identity moves from insight to impact.

Preparing for Every Next Season

In the next section, you'll be invited to move from reflection to action.

The exercise that follows isn't about fixing your spouse.
It's not about revisiting blame.
It's not about perfection.

It's about transparency with support from someone who loves the authentic you.

It's about honest assessment and intentional adjustment.

Think of it as your personal development camp.
A space to review your film, name your patterns, and begin designing a better emotional game plan—one that supports your leadership, your marriage, and your future.

Because knowing yourself is the beginning.
Governing yourself is how change happens.

Film Study of Self

FOR THE ATHLETE

(*Active, transitioning, retired, or rebuilding*)

You spend hours studying opponents, reviewing tape, and correcting technique. This exercise asks you to run film on *yourself*.

Locker Room Questions

Answer honestly. No performance. No pressure.

Who am I when I'm not competing?
(Beyond the jersey, title, or paycheck—what's left?)

What pressure brings out the worst in me?
(Injury, criticism, financial uncertainty, conflict
at home, transition?)

What emotional play do I run when I feel threatened or disappointed?

- I shut down

- I lash out

- I distract myself

- I avoid

- I overperform

What voice do I hear most in my head when I make a mistake?
(Is it coaching me forward—or tearing me down?)

What part of my identity needs development in this season?
(Leadership, communication, humility, patience,
purpose beyond sport)

Action Rep

This week, pause before reacting—at home, in
training, or in conversation.
Ask yourself: "Is this a reaction... or a response aligned
with who I'm becoming?"

That pause is emotional conditioning.

FOR THE SPOUSE

(Wife, partner, fiancée, or power-couple counterpart)

You manage transitions, emotions, schedules, expectations, and often everyone else's needs. This exercise invites you to check your own inner life—not just the household.

Locker Room Questions

Who am I outside of supporting someone else's calling?
(What parts of me need attention, rest, or growth?)

What emotional role do I default to at home?

- Fixer
- Peacemaker
- Silent supporter
- Over-functioner
- Emotional manager

What triggers my frustration or exhaustion most?
(Feeling unseen, instability, lack of control, uncertainty?)

What is my inner voice like when I'm overwhelmed?
(Gentle, critical, dismissive, demanding?)

- What would change if I gave myself the same care I give everyone else?

Action Rep

This week, choose one moment to speak truth instead of suppressing it—calmly, clearly, without apology.

Emotional maturity is not silence.
It's regulated expression.

TEAM HUDDLE (Read Together)

Answer separately, then share:

- One emotional habit I want to improve this season
- One way I want to show up better for myself
- One strength I bring to our team that I don't always acknowledge or share

You don't need perfection to build partnership.
You need awareness, honesty, and willingness.

Why This Matters

You can't manage what you don't recognize.
You can't grow what you won't name.
And you can't build a strong *we* until you understand the *me*.

This chapter wasn't about blame.
It was about clarity.

Next up: shifting from *individual conditioning* to *team strategy*.

CHAPTER 4

Who Are We? — Team Chemistry and Collective Purpose

We've looked inward—studying film on our own emotional and spiritual development, recognizing the importance of *self-examination* and *self-governance*. Now it's time to move from the individual locker room to the team huddle.

Because purpose doesn't stop with *who I am*—it expands into *who we are together.*

From Lone Star to Locker Room: Learning Team Chemistry at Home

Ray's Perspective

When Michelle and I first got married, I genuinely thought we made a great team—*as long as Michelle followed my lead.*

That was my mindset.

I came into marriage with the mentality I had learned in sports: someone's got to be the leader, call the shots, set the tempo. And in my mind, that someone was me. I had the platform, the career, the external success. So without even realizing it, I carried the same hierarchy from the field straight into our marriage.

> **What I didn't understand back then was that leadership without self-examination turns into control.**

I hadn't fully answered the question *"Who am I?"* as an individual, and because of that, I brought a lot of unexamined baggage into our relationship—assumptions about masculinity, authority, and what it meant to be "the head." I thought leadership meant direction without discussion. Vision without collaboration. Strength without vulnerability.

The problem wasn't that I wanted to lead.
The problem was that I didn't yet know how to lead with someone, not just over someone.

What I eventually had to confront—and what changed everything—was recognizing that even in our home, Michelle was also a leader.

And not just in a supportive role.

She brought insight I didn't have.
Perspective I couldn't see.
Emotional intelligence I hadn't yet developed.
Intellect, experience, discernment, and strategic thinking that—when I actually gave her room—made *me* better.

When I paused long enough to listen...
When I stopped competing for control...
When I allowed her leadership to complement mine instead of threatening it...

Our marriage didn't just feel better—it *performed better.*

That's when I started to understand something every champion-ship team already knows.

Great teams don't argue over titles.
They clarify roles.

They're honest about strengths and weaknesses.
They put the best person in the right position—even
if it challenges ego.
They rally around what serves the team, not individual pride.

When the team wins, nobody's worried about who gets the credit.

But when insecurity goes unchecked—when a man hasn't done the internal work to answer, "*Who am I?*"—it shows up as defensiveness, control, and resistance to partnership. And that blocks true cohesion at home the same way it would destroy chemistry in a locker room.

Looking back, I can say this with confidence:
If I had understood this principle earlier in our marriage—
the one Michelle is teaching so powerfully in this chapter—it
would have saved us years of unnecessary stress, conflict, and
emotional wear and tear.

That's why I'm sharing it now.

My hope is that if you're reading this early in your relationship, you'll avoid this pothole before hitting it. And if you're already dealing with this tension—power struggles, role confusion, unspoken resentment—you'll recognize it, address it, and recalibrate.

Because marriage isn't about who leads louder.
It's about who leads together.

And when two leaders learn how to function as one team—aligned in purpose, secure in identity, and committed to the mission—that's when real chemistry shows up.

At home.
For life.

Finding Our Position on the Team

Every athlete knows this truth: Talent matters—but positioning is what wins games.

The same is true in marriage.

There are two passages of Scripture that have consistently shaped my mindset, my posture, and my performance as a wife—and they functioned like a *playbook* for my marriage long before I had language for emotional intelligence or relational leadership.

The first is the book of Proverbs.

Proverbs was my early-season conditioning manual. It trained my decision-making, sharpened my discernment, and coached me on how to move with wisdom instead of impulse. As a young wife, it gave me moral instruction. As a woman of faith, it offered spiritual strategy. As a partner in a high-pressure marriage, it prepared me for real-life scenarios—some I hadn't even faced yet.

Reading Proverbs shifted my prayers. I stopped praying for ease and started praying for wisdom—the kind that protects a marriage, sustains a family, and carries you through seasons you didn't see coming.

Proverbs culminates in chapter 31 with the profile of a wife of character. And what stood out to me wasn't perfection—it was *performance under pressure.* This woman was strong, disciplined, intelligent, strategic, and resilient. She protected her husband's reputation, added value to his life, supported his leadership, and stewarded her household with excellence. She wasn't a sidekick—she was a *force multiplier.*

The second passage that shaped me was 1 *Corinthians* 13:4–7 (NLT)—a passage that became my relationship fundamentals drill:

Love is patient and kind.
Love is not jealous or boastful or proud or rude.
It does not demand its own way.
It is not irritable and keeps no record of being wronged.
Love does not rejoice in injustice but rejoices in truth.
Love never gives up, never loses faith, is always hopeful, and
endures through every circumstance.

That passage taught me how to love Ray through every season—winning seasons, rebuilding seasons, injured seasons, uncertain seasons, and transition seasons. It trained me in how to stay composed when emotions ran high, how to play disciplined defense when conflict threatened the unity of our team, and how to stay committed when circumstances tested our endurance.

These principles became tools we leaned on when navigating realities common in professional athlete households, including:

- In-law dynamics
- Family financial pressure and expectations
- Different money mindsets and spending habits
- Parenting under pressure
- Blended family challenges

- Transitioning from single to married behaviors
- And eventually, the shift into an encore career

These are baseline situations we now coach couples through in our *Performance Partnership Coaching*™ program. Scripture didn't just inspire us—it structured us. It gave us guardrails, strategies, and accountability for how we showed up as teammates.

Here's what I've learned:

Being on a team is a privilege.
Knowing your position is a gift.

> **When you understand and clearly define your role, you stop competing with your partner and start contributing to the mission.**

You add value that strengthens team chemistry instead of disrupting it.

When Ray was actively playing, my role was to be his emotional and mental support system—to help him stay grounded under the relentless pressure of maintaining a roster spot play after play, game after game, season after season. My assignment wasn't to critique his performance—it was to protect his peace.

When football was over, my role shifted. I wasn't called to pressure him for answers or criticize him for not having everything figured out. I was called to speak life into who he was becoming, not just who he had been on the field.

Roles evolve.
Seasons change.
But clarity is non-negotiable.

When roles go undefined, frustration fills the gap.
When roles are clear, chemistry develops.

Clarifying your position on the marital team is imperative. It's not optional—it's foundational. Don't skip this step. Don't assume alignment. Don't underestimate the power of understanding how you are meant to show up.

Because championship marriages aren't built on guesswork. They're built on intentional positioning, mutual respect, and shared execution.

When both partners know their role and honor the mission, the entire team wins.

There's No "I" in "Team": The Shift from Individual Ambition to Collective Purpose

There are countless books on discovering individual purpose, but very few that explore the *collective purpose of a marriage.*

That gap matters, because marriage doesn't exist to showcase two independent stars sharing a locker room. It exists to form a *team.*

When two people come together, God doesn't just merge two stories—He forms a new strategy. Marriage becomes the field where both partners' strengths, weaknesses, histories, temperaments, and callings intersect to build something far greater than either could accomplish alone.

In sports, no championship is won by individual talent alone. Even the most gifted athlete needs structure, chemistry, and shared vision.

> **Teams don't win because everyone plays the same position—they win because each person understands their role within the system**.

Marriage works the same way.

From Solo Performance to Shared Assignment

Before marriage, most of us are trained to think in "I" terms:

- My goals
- My career
- My dreams
- My timeline

And while personal ambition isn't wrong, it becomes incomplete once you enter a covenant partnership.

Marriage requires a shift from *"How do I succeed?"* to *"How do we win?"*

This is where many couples struggle—especially high performers. Athletes, executives, entrepreneurs, and leaders are conditioned to optimize personal performance. You're rewarded for independence, decisiveness, and individual excellence. But marriage calls for something different.

It calls for *shared strategy*.

Just as a sports organization recruits' players with unique skill sets to execute a unified game plan, God brings spouses together intentionally— not randomly—to complement, refine, and strengthen one another.

You weren't paired simply because you were compatible. You were paired because you were necessary to each other's growth.

Understanding the Team, You Joined

When you said, "I do," you didn't just say yes to love, companionship, or romance.

You said yes to:

- Alignment
- Accountability
- Adjustment
- Sacrifice
- Shared responsibility
- Long-term vision

You joined a team with an assignment.

That means your marriage isn't just about feeling connected—it's about *functioning cohesively*. It's about learning how to run plays together, cover each other's blind spots, and adjust when the game plan changes.

In every successful team:

- Someone leads
- Someone supports
- Someone adapts
- Someone stabilizes

- Someone challenges
- Someone protects culture

Sometimes those roles shift by season.
Sometimes one partner carries more weight.
Sometimes one partner needs recovery time.

But the goal never changes, *win together*.

I always tell the couples I coach this: *alignment matters more than agreement—but agreement is where alignment is proven*. Especially when decisions directly affect the health of your relationship.

Finances are one of the most sensitive areas of any marriage because money represents *security*. And security is foundational. For many women, security isn't about control—it's about stability, predictability, and trust. When that foundation feels shaky, everything else feels unstable.

When it comes to financial decisions—whether that's investing in a friend's startup, helping a family member financially, or taking on a major expense—those calls should never be made solo. A unilateral decision might feel efficient in the moment, but it creates misalignment that can cost you far more than money. It introduces friction, resentment, and emotional damage that's hard to quantify— and even harder to undo.

In marriage, you don't run separate drills.
You swim together.
You sink together.
You sail together.
You soar together.

When decisions are made as a unit, the outcome—good or bad—is owned by the team. If the investment doesn't pan out, or a family member misuses the support, you absorb the hit together. You recover together. You manage the emotional fallout together. That's what team chemistry looks like under pressure.

Security isn't just financial.
It's emotional.
It's mental.
It's physical.
It's relational.

If you're struggling to adopt a true *we* mindset with your spouse, don't just look at the behavior—*check the security gauge.* When someone doesn't feel secure, they can't fully commit to the play. They start protecting instead of partnering. Reacting instead of trusting.

You can't build championship chemistry on a cracked foundation. And marriages are no different. When spouses operate in opposition—making decisions independently, pulling in different directions—it threatens the very structure of the team.

Strong marriages aren't built on winning every call. They're built on *running the same play, trusting the same strategy, and protecting the same foundation.*

That's how teams last.
That's how marriages endure.

Here's the hard truth:
Individual success without relational alignment
eventually creates distance.

We see it all the time in professional sports:

- One partner is advancing while the other feels left behind
- One identity dominates while the other shrinks
- One dream is prioritized while the other is postponed indefinitely

Without intentional alignment, marriages drift into silent competition instead of collaboration.

But when couples shift from *me* to *we*, everything changes.

Decisions are no longer made in isolation.
Wins are celebrated collectively.
Losses are processed together.
Pressure is shared—not absorbed by one person alone.

That's when marriage becomes a *force multiplier* instead of a stress point.

Marriage as a Championship System

Championship teams don't just have talent—they have:

- Trust
- Communication
- Emotional regulation
- Respect for roles
- Commitment to the mission

That's why marriage demands emotional maturity and intentional partnership. Love may bring you together, but alignment keeps you together.

Marriage is where:

- Independence becomes interdependence
- Self-awareness becomes mutual awareness

- Personal growth fuels collective growth

And when both partners understand that they're building something bigger than themselves, the marriage stops feeling like a tug-of-war and starts functioning like a well-coached team.

A Kingdom Team with a Greater Assignment

For couples of faith, this goes even deeper.

> **Marriage isn't just a personal relationship—it's a Kingdom partnership**.

God didn't bring you together merely for comfort or companionship. He joined you to reflect unity, model purpose, and create impact beyond your household. Your marriage is meant to influence your children, your extended family, your community, your industry, and the people watching how you navigate pressure, success, and transition.

You weren't just drafted into marriage.
You were *assigned*.

And the moment you stop asking, "*What do I need?*" and start asking, "*What does this team need?*" you begin operating at a completely different level.

The Shift Begins Here

This chapter marks the pivot point of the book.

Up until now, we've focused on you—your identity, your inner work, your emotional development. That foundation matters, because healthy teams are made of healthy individuals.

But now the focus changes.

Now we move from:

- Self-study to shared vision
- Personal growth to collective purpose
- Individual goals to team mission

Because the strongest marriages aren't built by two people trying to win separately.

They're built by purposeful, *Performance Partners* who understand that when one wins, both win—and when one struggles, both adjust.

There's no "I" in "Team."
And there's no championship marriage
without a shared game plan.

Purpose and Drive: The Inner Athlete in Each of Us

To play at the highest level of any sport, you must be driven. The NFL accepts less than 3% of all college football players. Ray was one of the few. I watched him commit countless hours to the weight room, the playbook, and the grind—not just training his body but conditioning his mind.

That same drive that carried him from Eastern Illinois to the NFL became the fuel God used to strengthen our marriage.

> His story taught me something: **the discipline that brings you success professionally is the same discipline required to build a lasting marriage.**

But drive alone isn't enough. There were times when *my* drive faltered—when adversity felt like a closed door instead of a challenge to overcome. Where Ray saw resistance as motivation, I sometimes saw it as God's "no." Our different life experiences shaped how we handled pressure, disappointment, and success.

That's the power of partnership. God brought us together to blend those perspectives—his resilience with my reflection, his determination with my discernment. Together, those differences became divine balance.

Watch Your Film Study

When Ray and I started a deep dive, we began to see how our upbringing and personal habits impacted our partnership. We discovered where we mirrored each other and where we balanced each other out. That understanding became the foundation for a new level of unity.

Every team studies film—not just to evaluate the opponent, but to understand themselves. When you review your own relationship film, you're not looking for perfection. You're looking for patterns.

Take time to watch the "film" of your love story:

- How did you meet?
- What attracted you to each other initially?
- What strengths did each of you bring to the relationship?
- How did your backgrounds shape your expectations of love, communication, and conflict?

This kind of film study doesn't just clarify your purpose; it prepares you to show up, lock in, and perform when it matters most.

Mental Conditioning in Motion: From Awareness to Teamwork

We've focused on *self-examination* and *self-governance*. Next, we will build on the next two components of mental conditioning:

- *Relational consciousness*: awareness of how one's emotions, communication style, and behaviors affect others—especially intimate partners, teammates, family members, and colleagues.

- *Relational leadership*: intentional use of influence to create emotional safety, alignment, growth, and purpose within relationships and communities.

In marriage, this is where teamwork really happens. Relational consciousness is learning to read your partner's emotional cues like an athlete reads the field—knowing when to push, when to pause, and when to protect. Relationship leadership is executing the play—how you communicate, collaborate, and recover after a hard moment.

Couples with higher emotional capacity experience stronger communication, deeper trust, and longer-lasting satisfaction. Multiple studies examining emotional regulation and empathy in intimate partnerships suggest substantial gains in relationship resilience during stress, with some findings indicating increases of over 40% when these skills are consistently practiced (Halford, Pepping, & Petch, 2019). *Journal of Couple & Relationship Therapy.*

> **Emotionally intelligent couples play better defense— not against each other, but against outside pressure.**

Faith, Reflection, and Purposeful Partnership

Early in our engagement, Ray and I made a conscious decision that would quietly shape every season of our marriage: *we would be chain breakers.*

We didn't want to inherit patterns just because they were familiar. We didn't want to replay generational habits simply because they were modeled for us. We understood—even then—that love alone wouldn't be enough to sustain us. If we were going to build something that lasted, we had to be intentional about *how* we trained for it.

We studied.

We watched marriages around us the same way athletes study film. We paid attention to couples who communicated well under pressure—and those who crumbled. We noticed how some partners complemented each other's weaknesses, while others competed for control. We observed how unresolved pain showed up in conflict, how silence became strategy, and how avoidance often masqueraded as peace.

We asked questions.
We prayed for discernment.
And we began writing our own playbook.

That preparation became our *training camp*—the unseen work that would prepare us for the visible seasons ahead.

What we didn't fully realize at the time was how *different* Ray and I were—and how essential those differences would become to our purpose.

Learning to Value the Skill Set You Didn't Bring

Ray and I didn't come into marriage with identical temperaments, communication styles, or emotional wiring. Where one of us was decisive, the other was reflective. Where one was bold and vocal, the other was observant and intuitive. Early on, those differences felt like friction points—areas where we misunderstood each other or questioned motives.

But over time, we learned a critical truth that every successful team understands:

> **You don't build a winning roster by drafting clones.**
> **You build it by valuing complementary skill sets.**

In sports, a quarterback needs protection. A scorer needs a defender. A visionary needs a strategist. And a leader needs someone who can see what they miss.

Our marriage began to shift when we stopped trying to make each other play the same position and instead asked:

- *What does my partner bring that I don't?*
- *How does their perspective strengthen the team?*
- *What happens when I trust their role instead of resisting it?*

Ray's leadership sharpened my confidence.
My emotional awareness deepened his discernment.
His steadiness anchored my vision.
My insight expanded his impact.

What once felt like difference became *value*.
What once caused tension became *strategy*.

From Compatibility to Calling

Faith, reflection, and emotional examination helped us see our marriage not as a contract of convenience but as a calling of cooperation.

Marriage stopped being about who was right and became about what was right *for the team.*

We learned that purpose doesn't erase
differences—it assigns them.
It gives them direction.
It puts them to work.

Our marriage, our ministry, and this book are not accidental outcomes—they are the result of years spent learning how to:

- Listen without defensiveness

- Lead without domination

- Adjust without resentment

- Grow without losing ourselves

The goal was never perfection.
The goal was alignment.

And alignment requires reflection, humility, and the courage to let your partner's strengths cover your blind spots.

Purpose Is the Endurance Factor

What allows a marriage to endure seasons of pressure, transition, and change isn't chemistry—it's *clarity of purpose.*

That purpose becomes the stabilizer when emotions fluctuate.
It becomes the compass when decisions feel heavy.
And it becomes the motivation to keep showing
up when comfort fades.

Our commitment to faith and reflection didn't just strengthen us—it revealed why our partnership mattered beyond us.

We weren't just building a life together.
We were being prepared to help others discover the divine *why* behind their *we*.

And that's what purposeful partnership does:
It transforms differences into design.
It turns reflection into refinement.
And it allows two individuals to operate as a
unified team—on assignment.

Training Camp Exercise: Team Reflection

From Individual Film Study to Team Strategy

Every successful team pauses to review game tape—not just to celebrate highlights, but to understand patterns, chemistry, breakdowns, and opportunities for growth. This exercise is your chance to step into the film room together and study your story—not as critics, but as committed teammates.

This is not about blame.
This is about awareness, alignment, and intentional growth.

Phase One: Self-Examination—Reviewing the Film

Before you can adjust strategy, you have to see the plays clearly.

Individually, then together, reflect on the following:

How did you meet?
What season of life were you each in at the time? Were you in survival mode, growth mode, or discovery mode?

What values, habits, and emotional patterns did each of you bring into the relationship?
Consider family dynamics, communication styles, conflict habits, money mindsets, faith practices, and emotional regulation.

What strengths were immediately obvious—and which ones only became clear under pressure?
Who naturally leads? Who stabilizes? Who adapts quickly? Who needs time to process?

This is film study, not self-judgment. You're identifying tendencies so you can play smarter—not harder.

Phase Two: Self-Governance—Adjusting the Playbook

Once you see the patterns, the next step is deciding what stays—and what gets cut.

Ask yourselves:

Which emotional habits are no longer serving our team?
These are the plays that worked in earlier seasons but now cost you yards—defensiveness, withdrawal, silence, sarcasm, control, avoidance.

What reactions need to be retired from our playbook?
Just because a habit is familiar doesn't mean it's effective.

What new disciplines do we need to practice consistently?
This could include pausing before responding, naming emotions

instead of assuming intent, setting weekly check-ins, or praying together during tension instead of after it.

Self-governance is where growth becomes intentional. It's choosing discipline over default and strategy over emotion.

Phase Three: Relational Consciousness—Building Team Chemistry

Now you shift from *me* to *we*.

Discuss together:

How have our differences actually strengthened us—when we've used them well?
Where one of you is cautious, the other may be courageous.
Where one processes internally, the other brings clarity out loud.

Where do we need better awareness of each other's emotional signals?
What does stress look like for your partner?
Fatigue? Fear? Overwhelm?

What new plays do we want to install this season to strengthen team chemistry?
Think rhythms, rituals, communication cues, recovery strategies after conflict, and shared vision-setting.

Relational consciousness is learning to read the field together anticipating one another, covering weaknesses, and maximizing strengths.

Takeaway Thought

Your love story isn't random—it's strategic.
Every shared trial, every opposite tendency, and every
moment of grace has been part of God's design to align your
marriage with His purpose.

When you commit to understanding not just who you are, but
who you are together, you move from self-awareness to spiritual
teamwork—and that's where marriages start winning on purpose.

Purpose gives your marriage direction, but
focus gives it endurance.
To sustain what God builds between you, you must learn
how to balance the short game and the long one—on the
field and in your faith.

CHAPTER 5

Game-Time Focus—Playing the Long Game in Life and Love

Purpose points your marriage toward the goal while focus keeps you in the game. You can know who you are and who you are together, but without focus, even the most promising partnerships can drift off course. Focus is the difference between potential and performance. It's what keeps you grounded when life's pace quickens and distractions multiply.

Training the Mind Beyond the Game: Mental Conditioning That Extends Careers—On and Off the Field

Ray's Perspective

Making the jump from college football to the National Football League was one of the hardest transitions of my life. Coming from Division I-AA Eastern Illinois University, I knew the odds were stacked against me. The speed was different. The terminology was different. The expectations were higher. Every rep mattered. Every mistake was magnified.

There was an entirely new playbook to learn—new schemes, new language, new techniques. Footwork had to be precise. Assignments had to become instinctive. Conditioning wasn't optional; it was survival. If I wanted to make the roster—and, more importantly, *stay* in the league—I had to commit myself fully to developing my mental game. I studied film relentlessly. I stayed late. I trained early. I obsessed over details because at that level, talent alone isn't enough. Mental conditioning is what separates players who flash from players who last.

And while I was doing everything I could to sharpen my game on the field, there was another arena quietly being neglected.

My marriage.

I didn't see it at first. I *thought* I was present. I *thought* I was listening. I *thought* understanding an issue was the same as conditioning myself to change it. But those are two very different things.

I remember one moment vividly. Michelle was addressing a recurring issue in our marriage—something we had talked about more than once. As she spoke, I nodded. I responded. I gave verbal confirmation that I understood. But what I wasn't doing was prioritizing the work required to stop repeating the same mistake.

And then she said something that hit me harder than any coach ever had:

> "If you spent a fraction of the time you dedicate to being the very best football player you can be on the field on our marriage off the field, we would have a phenomenal relationship."

That was film review I couldn't ignore.

Every athlete understands this truth:
The game is won mentally before it's ever played physically.
The athlete who conditions their mind can perform under pressure without thinking. Repetition builds instinct. Discipline creates consistency.

Yet somehow, I had compartmentalized that truth—applying it to football but not to my marriage.

I had emotional wiring—habits, responses, blind spots—that had never been properly trained, challenged, or rewired. And just like poor footwork or lazy technique on the field, those untrained areas showed up repeatedly under pressure at home.

Here's the hard reality:
If you keep making the same mistake on the field,
you eventually get cut.

I realized I couldn't live with that same hypocrisy in my marriage.

I couldn't stand before God, my family, and my community and vow to love, honor, and cherish my wife, then refuse to do the uncomfortable, inconvenient work required to actually *become* that man. That level of integrity matters.

So, I committed to developing my mental conditioning off the field with the same seriousness I once brought to the game.

That meant therapy—doing the deep work, not just surface fixes.
That meant intentional prayer—not vague requests, but honest self-examination.
That meant accountability—giving trusted people permission to check me when patterns resurfaced.

That meant repetition—choosing new responses until they became second nature.

And I'll be honest: I'm still in training.

Mental conditioning is not a one-time drill—it's a lifelong discipline. But I can say with confidence that I've made tremendous progress from where I started. I show up differently now. I listen differently. I lead differently.

Looking back, I'm convinced that had I understood the importance of mental and emotional conditioning earlier in my career, I could have extended my playing years by three to five seasons. That's how powerful this work is.

But here's the win I'm chasing now:

I am determined to extend my career as a happily married man far beyond the final whistle.

Because championships don't only belong to athletes who last in the league—they belong to men and women who learn how to grow, adapt, and lead in their most important relationships.

I'm grateful for a wife who loved me enough to tell me the truth—and was patient enough to give me space to grow into it.

If you're reading this—especially if you're an athlete or high-performing leader—hear this clearly:

Developing your mental conditioning in your
relationship is not optional.
It's not soft.
It's not secondary.
It's not something you get to later.

It's how you stay in the game that matters most.

And the best time to start training...
is right now.

You train for seasons you can see—now prepare
for the ones you can't.
The same way you don't wait until game day to get in shape, you
can't wait until transition hits to build the skills you need for
your marriage, identity, and overall success.

The next six months matter.
Whether you're still playing, nearing retirement, already
transitioning, or fully transitioned, this is the window where
habits are formed, patterns are set, and outcomes are decided.

At Activating Intentional Marriages (AIM- Michelle's coaching
firm) we offer our clients a 6 month confidential process where
we walk them through our Performance Partnership Coaching™,
a private, elite, concierge experience designed specifically
for professional athletes and high-capacity leaders who
understand one truth:
*Longevity—on and off the field—requires intentional mental,
emotional, and relational conditioning.*

If you want to protect your legacy, strengthen your partnership, and
win the long game, *the time to train is now—not after the season ends.*

Formation: Studying the Couples Around Us

When we were still rookies in marriage, Ray and I made it our business
to seek out "veteran couples" the same way a young athlete studies
seasoned players on the field. We'd approach couples—newlyweds,
ten-year pros, even those married for 30 years or more—hoping to

get the wisdom we desperately needed for our own playbook. But instead of strategy, most of what we heard felt more like penalty flags.

Some shrugged and said, *"Don't do it."*
Others joked, *"The woman is always right—just accept it now."*
A few chuckled like marriage was a losing season you had to endure instead of a championship team you get to build.

Neither Ray nor I absorbed that rhetoric. It didn't sit right with our spirits or our vision. We were madly in love—still in that early-season momentum where you believe anything is possible. And we were determined to win. Not just survive. *Win.*

So instead of relying on the noise from the sidelines, we started doing our own film study.

We analyzed how couples talked to each other.
How they handled conflict.
How they supported—or ignored—each other.

We watched our families, too. We saw patterns that felt familiar but unhealthy, and we made a pact right there:

We were going to be chain breakers.
Anything—ANYTHING—passed down through generations that stalled growth, killed communication, or sabotaged love would stop with us.

We would break cycles with intention and rebuild patterns with purpose.
We weren't going to repeat bad habits just because they were modeled to us.
We weren't going to let emotional immaturity become the silent play caller in our home.

And we certainly weren't going to let negativity become the narrative of our marriage.

Our prayer—and our purpose—became crystal clear:

To become the best husband and wife we could possibly be
to and for each other.
To train like champions.
To love like teammates.
To fight for the legacy we wanted—not the legacy we inherited.

Our focus wasn't on the day-to-day frustrations.
Our focus was the endgame:

"Till natural death do us part."

Not as a cliché.
Not as a hope.
But as a strategic, disciplined commitment to the marriage
we were building—one rep, one decision, one emotionally
intelligent moment at a time.

Winning the Moments That Decide the Season

By the time we reached this stage of our marriage, Ray and I had already done a lot of the internal work. We understood the value of self-examination. We had learned how to self-govern—to pause, reflect, and take responsibility for our emotional responses. We were practicing relational consciousness—being aware of how our words, tone, and timing affected one another.

And yet, even with all that growth, we still found ourselves getting stuck.

Same arguments.
Same tension points.
Same emotional collisions—just different days.

It felt like running the same play over and over again, expecting a different result. We weren't clueless. We weren't careless. But we were missing something critical: *game-time focus.*

Because practice prepares you—but games expose you.

Conflict is game time for a marriage. It's where pressure is real, emotions are high, and instincts take over. And what we discovered is this: *no amount of self-work matters if you don't know how to execute differently when it counts.*

We didn't know how to stop the cycle, because we were both still reacting from familiar positions. Defending. Explaining. Proving. Retreating. Even when you're emotionally aware, old plays can still show up under pressure.

It took intentional, narrowed focus—one issue at a time—for me to recognize a hard truth:
one of us had to make a different choice if we wanted
a different outcome.

That "one" had to be me.

Not because Ray was wrong.
Not because I was superior.
But because leadership in marriage doesn't always mean authority—it often means initiative.

I had to surrender my ego.
I had to let go of needing to win the argument.

I had to humble myself enough to stop reacting
and start responding.

That meant getting ahead of the moment instead of getting dragged into it.

In sports, the best players don't just react—they anticipate. They read the field. They understand what's happening beneath the surface of the play. And that's what I had to learn to do emotionally. I had to elevate my perspective enough to see that what we were arguing about on the surface wasn't the real issue.

The real issue was often an unspoken need.
A fear Ray didn't yet have language for.
A pressure he didn't know how to articulate.
A disappointment he hadn't consciously processed.

And because he wasn't fully aware of it, he couldn't communicate it clearly. That's not failure—that's humanity.

Game-time focus required me to slow the moment down internally, even when the conversation felt fast and heated. It required me to ask myself different questions:

What's really being asked right now?
What's the emotion underneath this reaction?
What would leadership look like in this moment—
not control, but care?

This is where self-governance meets relational consciousness in real time.

It's one thing to know your triggers.
It's another thing to override them under pressure.

That override is what separates emotional growth from emotional maturity.

I began choosing responses that didn't come naturally at first. Silence instead of sarcasm. Curiosity instead of defense. Empathy instead of entitlement. Those choices weren't passive—they were disciplined. They were strategic. They were trained.

And slowly—but decisively—the dynamic began to shift.

Not because we avoided conflict.
But because we learned how to play it differently.

> **Game-time focus isn't about perfection. It's about awareness under pressure. It's about recognizing that the moments you're most tempted to protect yourself are the moments that require the most leadership.**

Marriage doesn't fall apart because couples don't love each other. It fractures because they don't know how to manage the moments that matter most.

And those moments—the arguments, the misunderstandings, the emotional stand-offs—are the plays that decide the season.

When you learn how to focus in those moments—how to regulate yourself, read your partner, and choose growth over ego—you stop replaying the same losses and start building real momentum.

That's game-time focus.

The Focus Factor: What You Lock In, You Become

In professional sports, focus isn't optional—it's survival. The ability to lock in, stay present, and execute under pressure separates those who simply play from those who dominate. Every snap, every swing, every second matters. Yet what most people never see is that this intense concentration isn't just about the game; it's about mastering your mind, emotions, and awareness.

Marriage requires the same discipline. The season may be different, but the pressure feels familiar. The focus it takes to maintain unity, protect peace, and pursue purpose under the spotlight of public life is no small task. The truth is, the same qualities that make you a professional at your craft can make you extraordinary in your covenant—*if you learn to apply them with intention.*

Because focus is not only about *what* you give your attention to; it's also about *where* your attention belongs and *when* it's needed most.

Focus is essential in life—not just *what* you focus on, but *where* and *when* that focus is needed. In professional sports, focus is everything. It's what separates those who merely compete from those who excel. At this level, intentional focus becomes a survival skill, because the average professional athletic career is short-lived.

I understand why so many athletes channel nearly all their energy into maintaining their position—the competition is constant, and the margin for error is small. The "short game" matters. Every practice, every snap, every play could determine a contract, a roster spot, or a legacy.

> **In life—and in marriage—the truly successful learn to play both the short game and the long game simultaneously. They compete hard in the present while planning for purpose beyond the season. That's strategy.**

Strategy: From the Field to the Family

In pro sports, careers are short—often just a few years at the top before new talent rises. That urgency fuels relentless dedication. You train harder, study longer, and perform under constant evaluation because one slip-up could cost you everything.

I understand why many athletes get tunnel vision, pouring every ounce of focus into their craft for fear of losing their spot. The short game matters—but the most successful players, leaders, and couples learn to play the short game *while preparing for the long one.*

The difference between burnout and breakthrough is balance.

The difference between temporary success and lasting legacy is strategy.

In chess, the world's best players—called Grandmasters—are celebrated for one reason: foresight. Their greatness doesn't come from reaction but from recognition—years of study, emotional composure, and pattern awareness. They can see five, six, even ten moves ahead.

Marriage demands the same mastery. You can become a *Grandmaster* of your relationship when you approach it with:

- Dedicated study of your marital design—not assuming you already know it, but continuing to learn your spouse's heart, needs, and love language over time

- Intentional experience—choosing to work through challenges rather than retreat from them

- Superior pattern recognition—noticing habits, tone shifts, or emotional cues that either strengthen or weaken connection

Mental conditioning becomes the key to this mastery. It sharpens your awareness, improves your decision-making, and strengthens your emotional endurance.

It is your playbook. It trains you to see the emotional "field"—your spouse's moods, needs, and stress levels—with clarity and compassion. It teaches you to manage your own emotions, so you can respond wisely rather than react impulsively.

Playing the Long Game: Mental Conditioning and Post-Career Success

In the locker room, everyone knows the truth: you don't win on game day without preparation during the week. Marriage works the same way. You don't build a strong partnership in the highlight moments—you build it in the daily reps. The way you manage your emotions, communicate under pressure, recover after conflict, and stay locked in when the season gets hard determines whether your marriage stays competitive or starts to fall apart.

> **The couples who last aren't the most talented or the most romantic—they're the most disciplined**.

They train their emotional awareness the same way athletes train muscle memory. They learn when to pause instead of react, when to listen instead of defend, and when to adjust instead of quit. That kind of conditioning shows up at home long after the noise fades. It creates stability, trust, and a partnership strong enough to carry a family through every season.

This is what championship marriages understand: love gets you in the game, but *performance keeps you there*. And performance, in marriage, is choosing to show up prepared—mentally, emotionally, and spiritually—every single day.

In relationships, focus is emotional regulation in motion—staying calm under pressure, staying present during conflict, and staying aware when distractions compete for attention.

When couples learn to "train their focus," they don't just react to life; they respond with intention. They learn to recognize the emotional "tells" in each other's language, tone, and body cues. They develop relational muscle memory—the ability to recover quickly from misunderstandings and reset as a team.

> **Working on your marital mental conditioning while building your athletic skill is not a distraction—it's a multiplier**.

It sustains your performance now and safeguards your purpose later. It's how focus transforms using discipline and discernment.

The Discipline of Focus: Knowing When to Lock In and When to Look Up

Focus in sports is about narrowing attention to the moment—the play in front of you. But focus in marriage is about expanding your awareness—seeing the bigger picture God is painting through your partnership.

- On the field, focus means blocking out distraction. In marriage, focus means *noticing* what you've been overlooking.

- On the field, focus means reacting fast. In marriage, focus means *responding thoughtfully.*

The best athletes learn that focus isn't about tunnel vision—it's about timing. You don't need to focus on everything all at once; you need to focus on the right thing at the right time.

Even Jesus modeled focus. Throughout His ministry, He faced distractions, critics, and competing demands, yet He remained locked in on His Father's mission. His rhythm was intentional withdrawing for solitude when needed, engaging with purpose when called.

Marriage, much like ministry, requires this sacred balance—knowing when to lean in and when to pull back, when to listen, and when to lead. Philippians 3:14 reminds us to *"press toward the mark for the prize of the high calling of God in Christ Jesus."* Focus is not just about the finish line—it's about being faithful in every yard of the field.

There are moments to lock in—to guard, grind, and protect your team.

And there are moments to look up—to reflect, recalibrate, and remember the long game you're building together.

Reflection Drill: The Focus Alignment

In sports, focus isn't accidental—it's trained. Players don't just show up on game day and hope their attention is sharp; they practice directing it. The same is true in marriage. Where your focus goes determines what grows. This drill is designed to help you intentionally align your attention, energy, and emotional awareness so your marriage isn't just reacting to life but leading it.

The Drill

Set aside uninterrupted time. Phones down. No multitasking. This is a *focus session*, not a surface conversation.

Ask yourselves these questions slowly and honestly:

Where is our attention most invested right now—our purpose, our problems, or our performance?
Be real. Are most of your conversations about logistics, stress, schedules, finances, and frustration? Or are you intentionally revisiting *why* you're together and *what* you're building? Focus reveals priorities, not intentions.

Are we overtraining for the short game while neglecting the long game?
The short game includes career demands, public image, money, parenting logistics, and daily pressure.
The long game includes connection, emotional safety, faith, trust, intimacy, and legacy.
Ask yourselves: *What season are we preparing for—this year, or the rest of our lives?*

How can we apply emotional intelligence to manage focus more effectively?
This is where mental conditioning becomes relational skill.

- *Examination:* What keeps pulling our focus away from each other?
- *Governance:* How do we manage stress before it spills into conflict?

Consciousness: What is my partner carrying that I may not be seeing?
Focus sharpens when emotions are understood instead of avoided.

What distractions need to be benched for this season?
Every team has to make cuts. Not everything deserves playing time.
Identify habits, commitments, mindsets, or outside voices that

are draining your energy and weakening your chemistry. Ask: *Does this move us closer to our purpose—or pull us away from it?*

The Challenge: The Focus Huddle

This week, schedule a *20-minute Focus Huddle*—no longer, no shorter.

Together:

Write one short-term focus goal
(*Something to strengthen right now—communication, patience, emotional availability, prayer, rest, or connection*)

Write one long-term legacy goal
(*Something you're intentionally building—marital culture, family values, spiritual leadership, generational impact*)

Pray over both goals together.
Commit to revisiting them *monthly*, the same way teams review film and adjust strategy mid-season.

This isn't about pressure—it's about alignment.

Closing Thought

In life, as in sports, focus determines direction.
But the greatest players—and the strongest couples—don't just master moments; they master *meaning*.

Becoming a *Grandmaster* of your marriage means studying it, strengthening it, and stewarding it with the same intentionality you give your career. When your focus expands beyond the immediate game to God's greater plan, you don't just play to win—you play to last.

Focus gives direction, but practice builds endurance. Champions aren't crowned in the spotlight—they're shaped in the quiet repetitions no one sees. And marriage is no different.

Once you learn how to focus your attention and align your energy toward purpose, the next step is to *practice it daily*. Every conversation becomes a rep. Every choice becomes conditioning. Every act of grace strengthens your form.

In the next chapter, we'll explore how to turn your faith, focus, and emotional awareness into consistent habits—the kind that build championship partnerships that don't just survive seasons but lead with legacy.

CHAPTER 6

Practice Makes Partnership— Building Championship Habits

Focus gives direction, but *practice creates transformation.*

The Unseen Reps: Where Championship Habits Are Forged

I remember watching Ray in college long before the NFL ever became a reality.

Everyone saw him at team workouts.
Everyone saw him at practice.
Everyone saw him on game day.

But what most people *didn't* see was the work he did when no one was watching.

Ray didn't just show up—he doubled down.

At Eastern Illinois University, he was already a two-sport athlete. His scholarship was originally for track and field before he walked onto the football team and earned his spot. That alone says something about his mindset. But instead of separating the two sports, he merged them. He took what he learned on the track—explosiveness, endurance, mechanics, discipline—and applied it to football in ways that gave him a competitive edge.

If there was a hill nearby, he ran it.
If there was time for one more rep, he took it.
If the team workout ended, his personal one didn't.

He created additional conditioning routines that weren't required. Extra sprints. Extra laps. Extra days. He invited teammates to join him, but most didn't—at least not consistently. The difference wasn't talent. It was commitment. Ray understood something early on that most people never fully grasp:

Championship results are built on habits no one applauds.

Watching him push his body—sometimes to exhaustion—gave me a front-row seat to how discipline compounds over time. It wasn't glamorous. It wasn't celebrated. But it was effective. Those unseen reps became the foundation that carried him into the NFL.

And years later, I realized something powerful:

The same habits that prepare an athlete for elite performance on the field are the same habits required to sustain excellence off the field.

What Ray was doing physically in college—training beyond what was expected, conditioning for what was coming, preparing for a future he hadn't reached yet—is the exact mindset couples need when building a marriage that lasts.

Great marriages, like great athletes, aren't
built on what's required.
They're built on what's *intentional*.

They're built in the quiet.

In the extra reps.

In the disciplines no one forces you to do.

That's where championship habits are formed—long before the spotlight ever shows up.

Every championship team understands this truth: greatness is never built in the spotlight. It's forged in repetition—in the quiet, disciplined work no one applauds, no one posts, and no one celebrates publicly. The greatest players, coaches, and leaders don't just know the game—they execute the fundamentals daily.

Marriage works the same way.

You can dream about a strong relationship.

You can pray for unity.

You can desire connection, peace, and purpose.

But without intentional practice, those dreams remain potential, not performance.

Healthy habits and intentionality go hand in hand. You can *want* to be an exceptional spouse, but without systems that support that desire, it stays stuck in intention instead of becoming transformation. Just like in sports, wanting to win doesn't win games—training does.

James Clear, author of *Atomic Habits*, says it best:

> You do not rise to the level of your goals. You fall to the level of your systems.
>
> Goals are good for setting direction, but systems are best for making progress.

In other words, habits are the practice plan of your purpose. Systems are how you run the plays that turn belief into behavior.

Up to this point, we've focused on the first three pillars of your mental conditioning framework:

- *Self-examination*—learning to study your own film
- *Self-governance*—choosing disciplined responses over default reactions
- *Relational consciousness*—becoming aware of how your emotions and behaviors impact your partner and your team

Now comes the fourth—and arguably the most visible—phase:

Relational Leadership

Relational leadership is where everything you've learned finally shows up on the field. It's when you put your Performance Partnership Coaching™ into play.

It's not about control.
It's not about dominance.
And it's not about being "right."

Relational leadership is about initiative.

It's choosing to model the habits you want to see.
It's setting the emotional tone of the relationship.
It's leading with consistency, humility, and awareness—
even when your partner is tired, guarded, or still
learning their own plays.

Every team has leaders who don't just talk strategy—they set the standard through repetition. They show up early. They stay locked in. They execute the fundamentals when the game gets tight.

That's what relational leadership looks like in marriage.

It's how love moves from feeling to function.
From theory to trust.
From intention to impact.

It's breaking down how to build championship-level habits—the daily practices that reinforce trust, deepen connection, and create stability across seasons of pressure, success, transition, and uncertainty.

In marriage, just like in sports, talent gets you noticed—but habits keep you winning.

> **When you commit to practicing love with the same discipline you bring to your profession, partnership stops being accidental—and starts becoming championship-caliber.**

From Goals to Systems: The Game Plan of Marriage

In athletics, setting a goal like *"win the championship"* fires people up—but no championship was ever won on motivation alone. Winning is the result of systems: early mornings, disciplined schedules, nutrition plans, film sessions, recovery routines, and accountability structures that show up long after the hype fades.

Marriage follows the same principle.

It's not enough to want a great relationship. Wanting connection doesn't automatically create it.

> **Wanting peace doesn't eliminate conflict. Wanting longevity doesn't guarantee endurance. What sustains a marriage—especially under pressure—are the systems that support it.**

Systems are how love gets practiced.

They are the daily rhythms of prayer, communication, reflection, repair, and reconnection that keep your relationship conditioned for the long haul. They turn intention into execution. They protect the marriage when emotions fluctuate, seasons shift, or life becomes unpredictable.

This is where *relational leadership* becomes essential.

Relational leadership means someone is always willing to step up emotionally—not to control, dominate, or win, but to *stabilize, clarify,* and *guide the relationship forward.* It's the courage to lead the marriage through structure when feelings are inconsistent. It's trusting the process even when progress feels slow.

Just like athletes trust training even when results aren't immediate, couples must learn to trust their systems—showing up, practicing consistently, and refining their partnership season after season.

Team Communication: The Locker Room of Love

Every elite team understands one truth: chemistry isn't accidental—it's communicated.

You can have all the talent in the world, but without clear communication, even the best players miss assignments, run the wrong routes, and lose games they should have won. Marriage is no different.

> **Strong marital systems are built through open, consistent, and intentional communication.**

This is your locker room—the space where you debrief, recalibrate, and prepare for what's next.

Relational leadership shows up here when couples commit to regular "team meetings"—intentional conversations where expectations are aligned, plays are refined, and progress is acknowledged. These aren't crisis talks; they're maintenance meetings.

What works for one partner may not work for the other—and that's not a weakness. That's diversity. The goal isn't uniformity; it's unity.

Healthy communication isn't just about exchanging information. It's about creating:

- Trust (I can be honest without fear)
- Transparency (Nothing is off limits)
- Emotional safety (Mistakes won't cost me the relationship)

That's the locker room of love—a place where accountability and encouragement coexist, where truth is spoken with care, and where both partners are coached toward growth instead of criticized into silence.

Mental Conditioning in Practice: Turning Awareness into Action

By now, you've done the internal work:

- *Self-examination*—understanding your patterns
- *Self-governance*—regulating your responses

- *Relational consciousness*—recognizing how your behavior affects the team

Now comes the execution of *relational leadership.*

This is where mental conditioning stops being a concept and starts becoming a culture.

A 2021 study published in the *Journal of* Personality and Social Psychology found that couples who intentionally practice emotional development habits—such as empathy exercises, reflective listening, and shared gratitude rituals—report higher relationship satisfaction and significantly lower stress levels.3

Why?

Because repetition builds reliability.

When you consistently 1) check in emotionally instead of assuming, 2) create safe spaces for honesty, 3) use grace-filled language during conflict, and 4) reinforce connection through daily rituals, you're building *emotional muscle memory.*

This is relational leadership in motion—choosing responses over reactions, alignment over ego, and understanding over control. Every repetition strengthens trust. Every consistent choice builds resilience. Over time, the relationship becomes conditioned to handle pressure without collapsing.

Building a Culture of Consistency

Strong marriages, like strong teams, are built on culture, not convenience.

Culture is what happens automatically when pressure hits. It's the sum of repeated behaviors that communicate what matters most.

In a healthy marriage, culture sounds like:

- "*Let's pray before we react.*"
- "*We don't ignore conflict—we address it.*"
- "*We protect our quality time like game day.*"

Those repeated behaviors form relational systems that reinforce emotional safety, empathy, transparency, and mutual respect. This is where leadership becomes shared—not positional, but relational.

> **When both partners model consistency, the marriage stops relying on mood and starts operating on maturity. Over time, intentional choices become instinctive partnership.**

That's the goal—not perfection, but *conditioning*.

Faith Integration: God and the Daily Grind

Spiritual growth and relational maturity are built the same way as athletic excellence—through discipline.

Scripture reminds us in 1 Corinthians 9:25: "*Everyone who competes in the games goes into strict training.*"

Athletes discipline their bodies for crowns that fade. Couples discipline their hearts for covenants that endure.

Every daily decision—to listen instead of interrupt, to pray instead of react, to serve without recognition—is part of your spiritual conditioning. These are not grand gestures; they are quiet reps. And over time, those reps compound into covenant strength.

Relational leadership means inviting God into the daily grind—not just the big moments. It's recognizing that faith isn't reserved for crisis; it's practiced in consistency.

The Leadership Shift That Sustains the Team

At this stage, marriage stops being about *who's right* and starts becoming about *what's required.* Someone must lead the relationship forward—and often, that leadership looks like humility, patience, and emotional steadiness.

Relational leadership is choosing the long game.
It's managing energy, protecting connection, and stewarding love with intention.

When you move from goals to systems, from awareness to action, and from individual effort to shared leadership, your marriage becomes more than strong—it becomes sustainable.

Because championships aren't won in moments.
They're built in systems.
And marriages that last don't rely on emotion alone—they rely on practiced, performance-driven partnership.

This is the moment where your mindset shifts—from *victim to victor*, from reaction to responsibility. This is what leadership evolution looks like.

True leaders don't wait for ideal conditions.

They don't lead from the sidelines, the bottom of the pile, or the place of blame. Leaders step forward first. They set the tone. They change the atmosphere by making choices that are not self-serving, but *team-serving.*

In every sport, the best leaders understand something critical: sometimes winning the game requires personal sacrifice. Think about the basketball player who intentionally takes a foul—not out of frustration, but out of awareness. He sees a momentum-shifting play developing. He knows giving up a personal stat or risking foul trouble is worth it if it stops the opponent from scoring, breaks their rhythm, or protects the team from a game-changing moment. That's not weakness. That's *high-level game IQ*. Marriage works the same way. Championship partners don't ask, "*What's fair?*" They ask, "*What's best for the team?*"

Sometimes leadership looks like being the first to apologize.
Sometimes it looks like regulating your emotions when you'd rather react.
Sometimes it looks like laying down your ego, your pride, or your need to win the argument so the relationship can win the season.

That's not losing yourself—that's *leading yourself.*

Whether you're the athlete or the spouse, this is your moment to shine. Leadership in marriage isn't about dominance or control; it's about awareness, sacrifice, and intentional action. It's about understanding that your choices—especially under pressure—either elevate the environment or poison it. And here's the truth: every marriage already has a leader. The question is whether that leadership is driven by ego or by purpose.

Champions sacrifice comfort for legacy.

They give up the short-term win for the long-term victory. They understand that the greatest leadership move is often the one that no one applauds, but that everyone benefits from. That's championship-level partnership. That's relational leadership.

Practice Drill: Building Your Championship Systems

Championship teams don't improvise their way to success—they install systems, rehearse them, and adjust them as the season demands. This drill is about moving your marriage from intention to execution.

Set aside 20 focused minutes together. No phones. No distractions. Treat this like a scheduled film session—not optional, not rushed.

Step 1: Film Review—What's Already Working

Ask yourselves:

- What daily or weekly rhythms currently help our marriage feel connected, steady, and supported?

- Where do we naturally communicate well—emotionally, spiritually, or practically?

- What habits make us feel like we're on the same team?

This step builds *self-examination* as a couple. You're identifying strengths before fixing weaknesses—just like a coach reviewing highlights before correcting form.

Step 2: Gap Analysis—Where Consistency Breaks Down

Now move into honest evaluation:

- Where are we inconsistent—not because we don't care, but because life gets busy?

- Do we tend to react instead of relying on rhythm?

- What conversations, routines, or emotional check-ins keep getting postponed?

This is *self-governance* in action. You're recognizing patterns without blame and taking responsibility for change instead of waiting for a "better season."

Step 3: System Design—Installing New Plays

Together, decide:

- How can we improve communication around routines, expectations, and responsibilities?
- What boundaries or adjustments would protect our time, energy, and connection?
- What one habit would make the biggest difference if practiced consistently?

Then identify *emotional conditioning habits* you want to add this month, such as:

- Daily gratitude (spoken or written)
- Short prayer or intention-setting together
- Weekly reflection or check-in
- Post-conflict debriefs instead of silent resets

This is *relational consciousness*—designing systems that support both partners and strengthen team chemistry.

The Weekly Challenge: One System, One Focus

Pick one system to develop this week—something simple, realistic, and repeatable.

Examples:

- A ten-minute morning or evening check-in

- A weekly date night or walk
- A post-practice or post-work debrief
- A shared devotional or reflection rhythm

Treat it like training:
Show up.
Refine the form.
Repeat the reps.
Adjust as needed—but don't quit the drill.

Closing Thought

Goals give you something to aim for, but systems give you something to grow through.

When both partners commit to intentional habits—grounded in love, faith, emotional awareness, and relational leadership—marriage stops reacting to pressure and starts moving with purpose.

Championship marriages aren't built overnight.
They're built day by day, choice by choice, rep by rep.

And just like in sports, no one wins alone.

Great partnerships are strengthened by the team that surrounds them—coaches who challenge, mentors who guide, teammates who sharpen, and communities that hold you accountable. You've learned how to focus. You've learned how to practice. You've begun installing systems that sustain your partnership.

Now it's time to step into the next layer of growth: *Who's in your huddle—and are they helping your marriage win?*

CHAPTER 7

Building Your Team—The Power of a Purposeful Circle

Your union was never meant to function as a solo act.

It was designed as a divine collaboration—with God at the helm and others alongside you for wisdom, accountability, and growth. As mentioned before, your marriage was created with *great purpose* in mind. God wants to use your relationship in a mighty way—to influence, inspire, and impact the world around you.

But even the most gifted players need a strong supporting cast.

Athletes don't train alone; they build ecosystems of excellence. Parents, coaches, nutritionists, trainers, mentors, and teammates form a network that pushes them from potential to performance. Each one is an *agent of change*—a catalyst for growth, development, and transformation.

Marriage operates by the same principle.

To become a championship couple, you must intentionally surround yourselves with voices and relationships that reinforce your values, challenge your comfort, and champion your purpose.

Building a Circle That Sharpens You—
Not One That Drains You

No one builds anything meaningful alone.

Not championships.
Not legacies.
Not marriages that last beyond seasons and contracts.

Every elite performer understands this truth instinctively: your environment shapes your execution. Who you train with. Who you listen to. Who has access to you when you're tired, frustrated, or unsure—it all matters. And in marriage, the circle around you can either reinforce your purpose or slowly pull you off course.

Scripture says it plainly: "As *iron sharpens iron, so one person sharpens another*" (Proverbs 27:17).

That verse isn't poetic—it's practical. Iron doesn't sharpen iron by being polite. It sharpens through friction. Through pressure. Through contact that makes both pieces better.

The people you allow into your life—your marriage, your home, your inner conversations—will either sharpen your discipline or dull your focus.

Teammates Are All Around Us

By the time Ray and I became acclimated to the new city, the new locker room culture, and the rhythm of being part of an NFL franchise, we finally felt like we'd found our tribe. Every team has its on-field roster—but off the field, there's a whole other team: the wives, the families, the circle that keeps the home side of the franchise functioning.

We found our chemistry with a small group of couples who attended the players' and couples' Bible study together. At the time, we were the rookies of the group—not in age, but in tenure. Everyone else had logged more seasons, more reps, more lived experience in this world than we had. And honestly, that worked in our favor.

The team chaplain's role was crystal clear. He coached us through biblical principles the same way position coaches guide players through fundamentals—footwork, technique, discipline. But the players and their wives played very different roles in our development. Each one brought a unique gift to the huddle.

There was the wife who knew every detail the team office ever released. Medical benefits, insurance policies, investment programs— you name it, she had the scouting report. She was the team's off-field general manager in my eyes. Looking back, I wish I had drawn closer to her sooner.

Another wife became my film study partner for biblical womanhood— she didn't just talk about submission, she lived it with grace, strength, and intentionality. I came from a single-parent home, and church was something I visited, not something that shaped me. I prayed often, but spiritual structure wasn't part of my upbringing. She helped me see submission not as silence or shrinking, but as strategy and stewardship within partnership.

Then there was the wife who showed me what it looked like to run a balanced offense—managing a husband, children, and a thriving career without losing herself in the process. She demonstrated a level of emotional intelligence that I didn't yet have the language for.

And truthfully? I learned from the other side, too. I observed women who were clearly struggling in their marriages, long before the public ever saw cracks. Even then, I sensed that purpose and pressure either grow a marriage or expose it.

Year after year, we watched God's purpose play out in the lives of many of those couples. We witnessed those But it wasn't until we moved back home and began serving at Ray's childhood church that we truly started to see the greater calling on our own marriage. It was like finally seeing the full field after years of running plays without understanding the entire playbook.

Leadership Under Control

In most high-performance environments, leadership is associated with authority, visibility, and control. But spiritually—and relationally—true leadership looks different. It starts with servanthood.

Not servanthood as self-erasure. Not as silence. Not as being controlled. But servanthood as strength under discipline.

Jesus flipped the script when He said, *"Whoever wants to become great among you must be your servant"* (Matthew 20:26).

In marriage and community, this means leading with humility, accountability, and responsibility. It means asking, *"How does my presence serve the growth of the people around me?"* It means recognizing that leadership isn't about being the loudest voice in the room—it's about being the most grounded one.

> **Strong couples don't just look for people who affirm them. They surround themselves with people who challenge them to be better—emotionally, spiritually, and relationally.**

Your Circle Is Always Coaching You

Whether you realize it or not, your circle is coaching you.

They're coaching how you talk about your spouse.
They're coaching how you handle conflict.
They're coaching what you normalize, tolerate, or excuse.

Some circles reinforce growth. Others reinforce dysfunction with humor, sarcasm, or shared frustration. Here's the hard truth: you don't rise above your environment—you adapt to it.

Scripture warns us clearly: "*Do not be misled: 'Bad company corrupts good character'*" (1 Corinthians 15:33).

That doesn't mean everyone around you needs to look like you, believe like you, or live exactly like you. But it *does* mean you should be intentional about who has influence. Because influence is never neutral.

The people you grew up with, your college buddies, and even your current teammates may be good people. They might be fun, loyal, and familiar, knowing exactly how to help you unwind after a long day. But here's the real question every leader has to answer at some point: Are they good *for* you?

Because when you level up—professionally, personally, or spiritually—you can't carry every relationship into the next season just because it played a role in the last one. Every athlete understands this truth on the field: what got you drafted won't necessarily keep you on the roster. The same applies to life.

As your responsibilities increase, your margin tightens, and your purpose sharpens, your surroundings must evolve. *Some relationships that once energized you may now distract you.* Some voices that once felt safe may now pull you off assignment. And some environments that helped you survive earlier seasons may quietly sabotage your growth in this one.

Relational leadership requires relational maturity.
It means having the courage to audit your circle—not with arrogance, but with honesty. It means recognizing that chemistry matters just as much as character, and alignment matters just as much as loyalty. Championship teams are intentional about who's in the locker room, who has access to the huddle, and who gets to speak into critical moments.

This isn't about cutting people off—it's about choosing wisely. Leaders understand that proximity is power. Who you allow close to you will influence how you think, how you respond under pressure, how you love your spouse, and how you lead your family.

Every season demands a different lineup.
And if you're serious about becoming who you're called to be—on the field and at home—it's time to make sure the people around you are helping you run your race, not slowing your pace.

Because growth isn't just about talent or opportunity.
It's about who's in your circle when the pressure is on.

Prepared to Lead—Even When You Didn't Ask To

One of the realities of growth—especially in marriage—is that as you mature, you automatically become a reference point for others, whether you want that responsibility or not.

There will always be people watching how you handle pressure. So ask yourself:

How do you speak to your spouse?

How do you recover from mistakes?

How do you manage success and disappointment?

Scripture speaks to this quietly but firmly: "*Encourage the young, be patient with everyone*" (1 Thessalonians 5:14).

Growth comes with responsibility. Not perfection, but awareness. God calls us to live in a way that creates space for those who are still learning. That doesn't mean you have it all figured out. It means you're willing to model honesty, growth, and accountability.

Your marriage becomes part of your leadership.

A Performance-Driven Circle

A *performance-driven circle* isn't built on proximity, history, or convenience—it's built on alignment.

> **Just because someone has access to you doesn't mean they should have *influence* over you.**

The right circle isn't impressed by your résumé, your platform, or your success.
They're invested in your character, your marriage, and your long game.

These are the people who:

- Respect your marriage, not just your wins, contracts, or visibility
- Call out blind spots without humiliating you—and challenge you without tearing you down
- Support your growth without competing for the spotlight

- Hold you accountable to the man or woman you say you're becoming, not the version that's convenient

- Protect your future even when it costs them access to your present

This kind of circle understands that success without stability is a liability.

They don't just show up for celebrations—they stay grounded with you after losses.
They help you process disappointment without self-destructing.
They remind you who you are when pressure
tries to redefine you.

Because real teammates don't just hype the highlight reel—they help you recover, recalibrate, and return stronger without losing yourself in the process.

So here's the real leadership test—one that requires honesty, not ego:

If your circle disappeared tomorrow, would your marriage be stronger... or more exposed?
Would your habits improve, or unravel?
Would your identity remain intact, or collapse under
the weight of silence?

The answer tells you everything you need to know.

Because the people you surround yourself with don't just influence your mood—they shape your mindset, your decisions, and your destiny.

And if you're serious about relational leadership, championship habits, and legacy-level living, then your circle must be as intentional as your training.

Alignment isn't optional at the next level.
It's required.

Why This Matters More Than Ever

Marriage is not just about who you chose—it's about who you *continue choosing to listen to*. In high-pressure, high visibility lives, the noise is constant. Opinions are loud. Expectations are heavy.

That's why building a performance-driven circle isn't optional—it's strategic.

You don't need more voices.
You need the right ones.

Because the strongest marriages don't just survive seasons—they are supported by environments that reinforce who they're becoming.

And when your circle is aligned with your values, your purpose, and your growth, you don't just endure the journey—you lead it.

Building Your Marital Support Team

Just as athletes select their circle intentionally, so should couples.

Here are key positions on your *marital roster*:

- *The Spiritual Coach*: A pastor, mentor, or faith leader who offers biblical guidance, prayer, and accountability
- *The Veteran Teammate*: Another couple a few seasons ahead who can model maturity and share lessons learned through real experience
- *The Training Partner*: Friends who encourage your growth individually and as a couple, keeping you spiritually and emotionally conditioned

- *The Coach or Therapist*: A professional "performance coach" for the soul—someone who helps you navigate emotional or relational blocks

- *The Cheer Section*: Family and friends who celebrate your wins and cover you in prayer when you take losses

The right circle doesn't just protect your marriage; it *propels* it. When you choose wisely, you create an environment that nurtures faith, focus, and fortitude.

Mental Conditioning and Relational Consciousness in Community

From a mental conditioning lens, this chapter moves us into *relational consciousness and relational leadership* beyond the couple. Your circle influences your emotions, mindset, and resilience more than you realize.

Research in the Journal of Family Psychology shows that couples who build and maintain supportive relational networks — including mentors, friends, and community ties — tend to experience stronger marital quality and lower stress during life transitions.4 Why? Because social support reinforces security and accountability.

Who you allow in your inner circle determines the health of your emotional ecosystem. Choose people who value confidentiality, encourage growth, and speak truth with love—not those who feed gossip, comparison, or criticism.

Play Action: The Impact of Visibility

With the platform of professional athletics comes a level of responsibility most people never carry.

Whether you asked for it or not, eyes are on you.
Your performance is analyzed.
Your lifestyle is discussed.
Your wins are celebrated.
Your losses are magnified.

And often without realizing it, your marriage is being watched too.

Professional athletes don't just represent a team or a city—they represent a possibility. People project their hopes, dreams, and assumptions onto you. They assume you've "made it." They assume the money solves everything. They assume life must be easy now.

But what many don't see is that visibility amplifies everything—not just success, but strain as well.

Visibility magnifies:

- Relational tension that was once manageable
- Unresolved childhood wounds that were never addressed
- Pressure at home that has nowhere safe to land
- Emotional blind spots that no longer stay hidden

It intensifies:

- Miscommunication that turns into chronic conflict
- Ego that blocks vulnerability and growth
- Silence that replaces honest conversation
- Expectations that outpace emotional capacity
- Performance at work while connection at home quietly erodes

It exposes the gap between who you are publicly and how you show up privately.

For many high-visibility couples, the damage shows up as:

- Emotional distance masked by busy schedules
- Resentment that builds underneath "being supportive"
- Spouses carrying the emotional load alone
- Identity confusion when the spotlight shifts or fades
- Conflict avoidance for the sake of image
- Intimacy becoming transactional instead of intentional
- Family decisions driven by optics instead of alignment

And when this pressure goes unchecked, it doesn't stay contained.

It spills into parenting.
It impacts mental health.
It distorts decision-making.
It fuels isolation.
It leads to burnout, detachment, infidelity,
depression, or divorce.

Not because people don't love each other, but because…

> … **love without emotional skill is fragile under pressure**.

Visibility doesn't create the cracks.
It reveals them.

That's why marriages in high-exposure environments don't fail from lack of love—they falter from lack of emotional conditioning, intentional systems, and relational leadership.

And that's exactly why this work matters.

And yet, that same visibility also creates a powerful opportunity.

Because when an athlete's marriage is healthy, intentional, and grounded, it disrupts narratives.

It challenges the belief that success ruins relationships.
It contradicts the assumption that fame and faith can't coexist.
It offers proof that love can grow even under pressure.

That's influence.

And influence always comes with responsibility.

Marriage as a Message—Whether You Intend It or Not

God's plan for your marriage was never limited to your household. He designed it to be a reflection—of commitment, of grace, of perseverance, of love that grows under pressure instead of collapsing.

Scripture tells us, "*To whom much is given, much is required*" (Luke 12:48). That doesn't mean perfection is expected—it means stewardship matters.

Just as Christ reflects the heart of the Father, marriage reflects something greater than itself.

When the spotlight finds patience instead of public chaos, humility instead of ego, unity instead of isolation, and growth instead of entitlement, people notice. Not because you're preaching, but because your life is speaking.

By year ten, Ray and I were in a completely different season.

Football was behind us, and we were learning how to reintroduce ourselves to the world beyond the game. We were reinventing who we were post-NFL, discovering our encore careers, engaging more intentionally in our community, and serving faithfully at our church.

Life looked quieter on the outside—but internally, we were more aligned than we had ever been.

That's when something unexpected started happening.

People we barely knew—sometimes complete strangers—began stopping us to comment on our relationship. Not because of Ray's former career. Not because of titles or platforms. But because of how we treated each other.

Some said they admired our affection—the way Ray held my hand, opened doors, or stayed present even in passing moments. Others shared how they longed to be treated with the same gentleness, patience, and respect they observed in him. A few women told me they loved watching the way I spoke to Ray, honored him publicly, and clearly trusted and respected him without shrinking myself.

At first, it caught us off guard.

We hadn't realized anyone was watching that closely.

But over time, it became clear—our marriage was speaking even when we weren't. Our relationship was communicating something powerful without a microphone, without a platform, without a spotlight.

That's when it truly hit us:

Our marriage was never just about us loving each other well.

It was about legacy.
It was about influence.
It was about showing others—especially those coming behind us—that healthy, intentional, purpose-filled partnership is possible.

We began to understand that the way we handled each other in everyday moments was leaving an impression far beyond our household. That our healing, our growth, our commitment to emotional maturity was creating a ripple effect in our community.

Our relationship had become a living example—not of perfection, but of intentionality. Not of image, but of substance.

That realization shifted everything.

We stopped seeing our marriage as something private to protect and started seeing it as something purposeful to steward. We understood that just like an athlete's career, our relationship carried influence—and influence always comes with responsibility.

That was the moment we recognized:
This wasn't just love anymore. This was leadership.

And once you see that, you can't unsee it.

Your marriage becomes a living testimony—an open invitation that says:
Healthy love is still possible.
Commitment still matters.
Faith and discipline still work.

And for young athletes, newly married couples, and families watching from afar, that matters more than you may ever know.

Influence Isn't Loud—It's Faithful

Influence doesn't require a microphone.
It requires consistency.

You don't have to host a marriage seminar.
You don't have to post perfectly curated moments.
You don't have to have it all figured out.

You simply have to be willing to live authentically.

God often works through proximity—through conversations in locker rooms, moments with teammates, casual questions from younger players, honest exchanges between spouses at events.

The ripple effect starts small.

A teammate notices how you speak about your spouse.
A younger player watches how you handle conflict.
A wife asks how you navigated a hard season.
A couple realizes they're not alone because you
were willing to be real.

That's how faith moves from belief to action.

James 2:17 reminds us that faith without action is incomplete—not because belief isn't enough, but because faith is meant to move. It's meant to show up in real choices, real relationships, and real integrity.

Run the Play You're In

You don't need a bigger platform.
You're already playing on one.

You don't need a flawless highlight reel.
You need integrity in real time.

Championship influence doesn't start when the lights get brighter—it starts with how you execute the play that's in front of you *right now*.

Start where you are.
In your home.
In your marriage.
In your daily decisions.

Look around your current huddle.
Who's already been assigned to your life in this season?
Who's watching—not to criticize or compete, but to learn what healthy partnership actually looks like?

Lead without performing.
Mentor when invited, not when applauded.
Share your story when it serves growth, not ego.
Step in when needed. Step back when it's not your assignment.

That's real leadership.

The truth is impact works like momentum. You don't force it—you build it. Small, consistent choices compound over time. Patience over pride. Unity over control. Humility over image. Those decisions don't always make headlines, but they change outcomes.

And here's what most people miss: You may never see the full reach of your obedience.

The couple who watches how you resolve conflict.
The teammate who notices how you honor your spouse.
The young athlete who realizes there's another way to win—one that doesn't cost him his family.

That's ripple-effect leadership.

Scripture puts it simply: "*Do not grow weary in doing good, for at the proper time you will reap a harvest if you do not give up*" (Galatians 6:9). Translation: Stay disciplined. Stay consistent. Stay in position.

You focus on executing with excellence.
God—and life—will take care of the reach.

Because legacy isn't built by chasing influence.
It's built by stewarding responsibility—one play, one season,
one marriage at a time.

Team Drill: Evaluating Your Circle

In sports, no athlete succeeds alone. Every elite performer has a circle
that sharpens their skill set, challenges their blind spots, and supports
them through seasons of pressure. Your marriage is no different.

> **The people you allow into your inner circle will either
> strengthen your partnership or subtly strain it.**

This drill is about *intentional roster management*. Not everyone
deserves courtside access to your marriage.

Reflection Questions

Take time to discuss these questions honestly and without defensiveness:

Who currently makes up our inner circle?
Who gets consistent access to your life, your
struggles, and your wins?

How does each relationship influence our growth?
Do they encourage maturity, accountability, and purpose—or do
they normalize dysfunction, negativity, or complacency?

Do our closest relationships align with the direction we're
headed—or the season we're trying to leave?

Some people are great for training camp but not built
for championship runs.

Who challenges us to be better, both individually and together?
Not just people who affirm you, but people who sharpen you.

Who do we need in this next season?
A mentor couple? A spiritually grounded friend? A peer who
understands the pressures of visibility, transition, or leadership?

Who might need to be moved from the starting
lineup to the bench?
This doesn't mean cutting people off harshly—it means
redefining access and influence.

Who are we being for others?
Are we modeling healthy partnership, emotional maturity, and
integrity for those coming behind us?

Challenge: Together, pray for clarity and discernment.
Then:

1. Write down five people or couples who consistently build
   you up, challenge your growth, and respect your values.

2. Write down one or two relationships that feel draining,
   misaligned, or counterproductive to where God is
   taking your marriage.

3. Discuss boundaries, not from a place of fear, but from wisdom.

Remember:
Boundaries aren't rejection—they're protection.
They guard your focus, your peace, and your purpose.

Closing Thought

Every great team is shaped by who's in the huddle.

Athletes don't rise to greatness on talent alone—they rise through the training, feedback, discipline, and belief of the people surrounding them. The same is true for your marriage.

God has intentionally positioned people around you to refine you, restore you, and ready you for greater impact. When you build your circle wisely, your relationships become reinforcements instead of distractions.

When your circle is strong, your marriage becomes more than a partnership—it becomes a platform.
A living example.
A source of hope.
A ministry in motion.

Build wisely. Because your circle will either carry you toward your calling or pull you away from it.

CHAPTER 8

The ROI of Relationship—Why This Book Matters for the Pro Athlete and Spouse

"We're learning that emotional intelligence is an important ingredient in helping professional athletes live healthy and successful lives."

—Gene Upshaw (Hall of Famer and former Executive Director of the NFLPA)[5]

The Why Behind the Playbook

If you're an elite athlete—or the spouse of one—you know this truth: excellence is won on the margins. It's not just about strength or speed, but consistency. It's not just about performance, but durability. This book isn't just a manual for being a good spouse; it's a strategic investment in your legacy, your career, your marriage, and your life.

You hear about athletes achieving greatness on the field, but too often you hear about the off-field fallout—marriages gone, finances broken, identity lost when the final whistle blows. The stakes are high. The clock is short. That's why this book is essential. Because your relational game—your marriage—affects everything else: your mental health, your focus, your team chemistry, your long-term career trajectory and beyond.

The Data Doesn't Lie: Emotional Intelligence Drives Performance Outcomes

Let's dig into the numbers. Multiple meta-analyses and peer-reviewed studies show that emotional intelligence (EI or EQ)—the ability to identify, understand, manage emotions and relationships—is a performance multiplier. This isn't fluff. This is competitive advantage:

- A large meta-analysis of more than 50,000 participants found that EI significantly predicts salary, career decision-making self-efficacy, career satisfaction, and turnover intentions.[6]

- In sports specifically, athletes with higher EI display better self-control, better emotional regulation, and more sustained careers—especially in high-pressure, contact, or referee-intensive sports.[7]

Research on the coach–athlete relationship shows that when athletes feel supported, understood, and connected to their coaches, they develop stronger emotional intelligence—which ultimately leads to better team performance. In short, healthier relationships build better athletes and stronger teams.

Put simply: if you develop relational skills (self-examination, self-governance, relational consciousness, relational leadership), your career (i.e. your relationship with your coach/player) and your marriage both win.

Linking Performance, Marriage, and ROI

Here's how all of this connects for you as a professional athlete and spouse:

- On-field performance: Mental conditioning enhances the ability to stay calm under pressure, bounce back from mistakes, and read opponents and teammates—so you remain at elite level longer.

- Off-field performance: Your marriage is your primary "team behind the scenes." A healthy partnership stabilizes your mind, supports your focus, and protects you when the game changes or ends.

- Post-career value: The average pro career is short. But the value of your marriage (and relational leadership) is lifelong. Couples who develop relational intelligence together often avoid the pitfalls many athletes face—divorce, financial collapse, substance dependence. Gene Upshaw's advocacy emphasized that developing emotional intelligence helps professional athletes build healthier, more sustainable lives beyond competition.

- Financial and relational ROI: A stable marriage can mean fewer distractions, improved decision-making, and consistent support—leading to better brand value, business ventures, transition opportunities, and legacy building. Data proves that EQ correlates to higher salary, commitment, and career adaptability.[8]

Investing in your marriage is not a side-project—it's a core part of your professional strategy.

The Championship Standard: Principles That Separate Strong Marriages from Strained Ones

1. Relational ROI is quantifiable. Emotional intelligence isn't just touchy-feely—it predicts real career outcomes, relational stability, and post-career success.

2. *Marriage is a performance asset, not a liability.* The better your partnership, the stronger your brand, focus, and longevity.

3. You play as a team—and your spouse is your MVP. When she (or he) is emotionally intelligent, aligned in purpose, growing in awareness, you both win.

4. Timing counts: The earlier you invest relationally, the more durable your career and legacy become.

5. This work matters for purpose and for profit—not just financial profit, but relational, spiritual, and community impact profit.

The Guiding Light of ROI and Mission

Every person has a guiding light—a phrase, a moment, or a person whose presence inspires them to keep pushing toward the goal. For some, it's the coach who saw potential when no one else did. For others, it's a verse, a prayer, or a defining moment that shifted perspective. That same guiding light that propels an athlete to greatness is the same spark that God uses to shape your marriage's mission. Your story together isn't random—it's intentional. Every trial, triumph, and turning point was designed to reveal the "why" behind your union. And now, it's time to bring that into focus—to identify the light that guides your partnership and write the statement that will lead your home.

In business, return on investment is the ultimate measure of effectiveness. Every system, every strategy, and every decision is designed to produce a result—to generate growth, impact, and sustainability. The same principle applies to relationships. The work you've done up to this point—developing self-awareness, emotional intelligence, focus, teamwork, and systems—has been about creating *relational* ROI: the tangible return that comes from investing wisely in your marriage.

When couples cultivate emotional intelligence, build healthy systems, and align purpose, the return is measurable. Strong marriages yield greater career longevity, lower stress, better decision-making, and increased life satisfaction. That's not coincidence—it's the compounding effect of consistent investment. Just as Fortune 100 companies maximize their ROI through mission clarity, healthy couples build the same return through shared purpose. Mission is what turns intention into impact.

When ROI and mission work together, you don't just survive—you scale. A business with a clear mission grows faster because every resource has direction. A marriage with a clear mission thrives because every effort has meaning. Both require vision, accountability, and alignment.

Reflection and Action: Measuring the ROI of Your Marriage

In professional sports and elite careers, everything is evaluated through return on investment. Time, energy, training, money, and focus are all tracked because leaders understand this truth: what you don't measure, you can't manage—and what you don't manage, you can't sustain.

Marriage is no exception.

Your relationship is not separate from your career—it is directly connected to how well you perform, recover, lead, and transition. A healthy marriage multiplies capacity. A strained one silently drains it. This section invites you to step out of autopilot and begin evaluating your marriage with the same intentionality you give your profession.

Creating Winning Stats That Matter

Take time—individually first, then together—to honestly reflect on these questions:

What does relational ROI mean for us?
Not just emotionally, but practically. How does our marriage impact our focus, decision-making, stress levels, leadership, and long-term vision?

How well are we investing in emotional intelligence— individually and as a couple?
Are we growing in self-awareness, emotional regulation, empathy, and communication—or relying on talent, chemistry, or avoidance to carry us?

Which areas of our relationship are producing value—and which are draining it?
Where do we experience clarity, connection, and support?
Where do we experience recurring tension, miscommunication, or emotional fatigue?

How do we want our marriage to function 10, 20, or 30 years from now—beyond game day?

What kind of partnership do we want when the lights dim, the schedule slows, or the platform shifts?

These questions aren't meant to create pressure—they're meant to create perspective.

Practice Plan: Turning Awareness into Execution

Reflection without action doesn't produce growth. Just like film study must lead to adjustments on the field, insight must lead to implementation at home.

1. Schedule a "Relational KPI" (Key Performance Indicators) Review

Set aside intentional time—quarterly or biannually—to review your marriage like a performance check-in.

Define 2–3 key relational metrics you both care about, such as:

- Communication satisfaction
- Conflict recovery time
- Emotional safety and trust
- Stress regulation and support
- Alignment in decision-making

Discuss where you're strong, where you're inconsistent, and where growth is needed—without blame, just clarity.

2. Choose One Relational Habit to Train This Quarter

Pick one simple, sustainable habit that strengthens your marriage *and* supports your professional performance, such as:

- A weekly alignment huddle
- A post-conflict recovery routine
- A daily emotional check-in
- A protected weekly connection window

Treat it like training:
Show up.
Track progress.
Refine as needed.
Repeat.

Consistency beats intensity every time.

3. Revisit Your "Why" for Marriage

Marriage was never meant to be just romance, convenience, or role fulfillment—it was meant to be purpose and partnership.

Together:

- Write down your shared "why" for marriage
- Define the mission of your partnership
- Align your household culture around that purpose

Return to it when pressure rises, seasons shift, or priorities compete.

Team Captain Perspective

Your career has KPIs.
Your finances have benchmarks.
Your body has conditioning metrics.

Your marriage deserves the same respect.

When you invest intentionally in mental conditioning and relational systems, your marriage stops being reactive and starts becoming a strategic asset—one that strengthens your performance today and secures your legacy tomorrow.

Because the strongest couples don't just win seasons.
They build futures.

Closing Thought

You've trained your body, sharpened your skills, studied your competition. But now the greatest edge you have may come from your relationship game. Because when your marriage is aligned, emotionally intelligent, and on-purpose, you don't just *compete*—you *dominate*. Not just for the next contract—but for life beyond the jersey.

So as we step into the final chapter, ask yourself:

- What is the mission that gives our marriage direction?

- How do we measure the return on what we've invested in one another?

- What guiding light, phrase, or moment keeps us anchored when life gets loud?

Because every successful organization—and every successful marriage—starts with one defining statement: the *"why."*

In the next chapter, you'll create your own *Marriage Mission Statement*—a clear, faith-anchored declaration of purpose that guides how you build your home, make decisions, and reflect God's love to the world. When your mission aligns with His, the return isn't just emotional or spiritual—it's transformational.

CHAPTER 9

The Mission of Us—Crafting Your Marriage Playbook

"Where there is no vision, the people perish" (Proverbs 29:18)

Clarity of vision and purpose — not just goal setting — is what sustains high-performing organizations.

Every world-class organization and every championship team operate from a clear mission. It's what defines how they work, decide, and win. Their mission isn't just words on a wall—it's a compass for culture.

Marriage deserves that same intentionality. Your relationship is the most important team you'll ever play on, and your home deserves the same strategic clarity Fortune 100 companies use to sustain excellence. Just as a business mission statement defines its purpose and priorities, a *Marriage Mission Statement* defines the spiritual and emotional identity of your union—what you stand for, what you value, and how you serve God and each other.

Faith and Vision: The Kingdom Perspective

God is a strategist. Every relationship He ordains carries a purpose. He brought you together not just to *do life* but to *change lives*.

Your marriage is meant to reflect His covenant—a living testimony of grace, strength, and unity.

Ephesians 2:10 reminds us, *"For we are His workmanship, created in Christ Jesus for good works, which God prepared in advance for us to do."* Your marriage is part of that workmanship—designed for impact, not accident.

When you define your mission as a couple, you're not just writing words—you're declaring alignment with heaven's blueprint.

Why Mission Matters More Than Motivation

Motivation fades. Mission sustains.

Athletes know this truth well. The drive that wins one game won't carry you through a season. It's the deeper *why*—the mission behind the training—that builds consistency, character, and championship habits.

In marriage, mission is what keeps you aligned when emotions fluctuate. It's the lens that filters decisions, guides forgiveness, and fuels growth. And just like in business, when your mission is clear, your ROI becomes predictable—peace increases, conflict decreases, and connection compounds.

Purpose with a Plan

In the professional world, no great company thrives by accident. They build a culture that reflects their mission. Google values innovation. Chick-fil-A prioritizes service. Apple thrives on simplicity and creativity. Each of these companies recruits, trains, and measures success based on alignment with their mission.

Strong marriages do the same.

> **When you define your mission, you create alignment in your home—clarity about what matters most and accountability for how you live it out. A marriage without mission is like a team without a playbook: talented, but unfocused.**

This isn't about perfection; it's about purpose. Your mission statement becomes the north star of your relationship, guiding how you communicate, recover, grow, and serve together.

Creating a Culture at Home

Building a culture of purpose requires intentional systems—just like we discussed in chapter 4. Companies create "culture handbooks"; teams create "codes of conduct." Your marriage deserves a "covenant culture."

That culture begins with a shared mission.

When both partners know the "why," everything else flows—the tone of your home, the way you handle conflict, how you raise your children, how you give, serve, and lead.

This is how you turn your marriage into a spiritual Fortune 100—anchored in clarity, consistency, and Christ.

Your Guiding Light

Think back to your defining moments as a couple.

- What was the moment that tested your faith but strengthened your foundation?

- Who or what has inspired you to keep showing up, even when it was hard?

- What phrase or scripture has carried you through challenges?

These moments are not random—they are divine breadcrumbs. They form the spiritual DNA of your marriage. Proverbs 20:24 reminds us, "*A person's steps are directed by the Lord. How then can anyone understand their own way?*"

The truth is your guiding light—God's hand at work in your story—is what will direct your next play.

Reflection: The ROI of a Mission-Driven Marriage

Before you write your statement, consider:

- What have we learned from our past chapters about self-awareness, teamwork, focus, and systems?

- How can those lessons translate into the long-term return of a purposeful marriage?

- What has been our greatest return so far—peace, partnership, growth—and how can we multiply it?

Your Marriage Mission Statement will be the spiritual and strategic foundation of everything that follows—a covenant that ties your purpose to measurable fruit.

Why Do You Think God Brought You Two Together?

This question is the heartbeat of your mission. God doesn't pair people randomly—He partners them with purpose.

Ask yourself:

- How has our story revealed God's grace?
- What Kingdom impact could our unity create?
- How can our marriage model faith, forgiveness, and fortitude for others?

Just as athletes trust their coaches' play calls, we must trust that God called this union for more than companionship—He called it for impact.

When you step back and view your relationship through this lens, you realize your marriage is not just *for* you—it's *through* you. God wants to reach others by reflecting His love through your covenant.

Next: In the following section, you'll walk step-by-step through crafting your *Marriage Mission Statement*—a declaration of purpose that defines your values, directs your culture, and delivers long-term relational ROI.

Step-by-Step: Writing Your Marriage Mission Statement

This process takes reflection, honesty, and collaboration. Set aside dedicated time, free from distractions, and treat this like a team meeting.

Step 1: Reflect on Your Journey

Review what you've discovered from previous chapters:

- Who are you individually?

- Who are you together?
- What are your shared values?
- How has God used your differences to strengthen your union?

Step 2: Identify Your Core Values

List 3–5 values that represent your shared foundation (examples: faith, grace, communication, service, growth, integrity, fun). These are your "pillars."

Step 3: Define Your "Why"

Complete this sentence together:

"We believe God brought us together to."

Don't rush it—talk it through. Revisit your defining moments and guiding lights.

Step 4: Envision Your Impact

Ask: How do we want our marriage to impact our family, community, and legacy? Consider how your relationship can be a testimony of God's faithfulness in real life.

Step 5: Write Your First Draft

Combine your reflections into 2–4 sentences that capture your heart and direction. Example:

"Our mission is to honor God through our marriage by serving one another in love, leading with integrity, and living our purpose with joy and discipline. We commit to building a home rooted in grace, truth, and unity so that others may see Christ through us."

Step 6: Revisit and Refine

Your mission will evolve as you grow. Review it annually—pray over it, adjust it, and recommit to it. Just like a team updates its strategy each season, your relationship will strengthen through continuous reflection and alignment.

Reflection and Challenge

1. What is our guiding light—the verse, phrase, or person that fuels our faith and focus?

2. What values define our partnership?

3. How do we want others to experience God through our marriage?

4. How can we live this mission out daily—in speech, service, and sacrifice?

Assignment:

Write your Marriage Mission Statement, frame it, and post it somewhere visible in your home. Make it part of your family culture, your dinner conversation, your prayer time. Let it become the code you live by—the vision that drives your love.

The Four Pillars That Changed the Game

Throughout this journey, you've been introduced to a mental conditioning framework designed to strengthen not just your marriage, but your leadership, longevity, and life beyond the game.

Let's bring it all together.

1. Self-Examination—Watching Your Own Film

This is where growth begins.

You learned to study your patterns, triggers, wounds, and defaults with honesty instead of shame. You stopped blaming circumstances and started understanding yourself. Like any elite performer, you realized that improvement starts with awareness.

2. Self-Governance—Making Different Choices Under Pressure

Awareness alone isn't enough. You learned how to regulate your emotions, manage your reactions, and choose responses that align with who you're becoming—not who you used to be. This is discipline. This is maturity. This is leadership of self.

3. Relational Consciousness—Seeing Beyond Yourself

You learned to recognize how your inner world affects your spouse, your home, and your partnership. You became aware of emotional dynamics, power shifts, unspoken needs, and shared responsibility. Marriage stopped being "me versus you" and became **us versus the issue**.

4. Relational Leadership—Setting the Culture of Your Marriage

This is where championship marriages separate themselves. Relational leadership means you don't just react—you *set the tone*. You model emotional intelligence. You protect the culture. You lead with humility, vision, and accountability. You understand that influence starts at home before it ever reaches the public.

Together, these four principles form a *high-performance operating system* for marriage.

Why This Matters—Especially for Professional Athletes

For professional athletes and high-visibility leaders, the return on this work is undeniable.

A strong marriage:

- Improves focus and emotional regulation
- Stabilizes identity during career transitions
- Protects against burnout, isolation, and destructive coping
- Strengthens decision-making under pressure
- Increases longevity—professionally and personally

This is relational ROI.

When your marriage is aligned, your life performs better.
When your home is healthy, your leadership expands.
When your purpose is clear, your platform becomes powerful.

Completing this book wasn't just about strengthening your relationship—it was about securing your future beyond contracts, seasons, and scoreboards.

Your Legacy Starts Here

Legacy isn't something you arrive at—it's something you're actively building. It doesn't begin at retirement, at a milestone anniversary, or when the pressure finally eases. Legacy starts here, in the choices you make today, the habits you repeat, and the way you respond in every season of marriage.

At the time of this writing, Ray and I will have been married for thirty years and together for thirty-four. Those numbers represent more than longevity—they represent lived seasons. Seasons of preparation and pressure. Seasons of clarity and recalibration. Seasons where growth was intentional and seasons where it was required.

We've navigated six years in the NFL as player and wife—an environment defined by extreme highs, sudden transitions, public wins, and private adjustments. We spent five years serving as chaplains for the Chicago Bears, walking alongside others while continuing to do our own internal work. We've parented four beautiful children into young adulthood, learning that every stage of parenting demands a deeper level of emotional intelligence and partnership. We planted a church for three years, discovering that leadership stretches not only capacity but character.

And then there are the seasons no one sees—the quiet years of failing forward, unlearning unhealthy patterns, rebuilding trust, strengthening communication, and choosing growth when comfort would have been easier.

Through every season, our marriage required *conditioning*.

Not just love—but endurance.
Not just commitment—but focus.
Not just faith—but emotional discipline.

Marriage, much like an athletic career, moves in seasons. There are training seasons, peak seasons, injury seasons, transition seasons, and rebuilding seasons. Each one demands a different mindset and a willingness to adapt without abandoning the assignment.

My mental conditioning framework wasn't created in theory—it was forged through experience. Self-awareness became my film study. Self-management became my recovery strategy. Focus became the discipline that sustained us when motivation dipped. Purpose kept us aligned when circumstances shifted.

Ray and I didn't get everything right—but we stayed intentional. We remained teachable. We learned how to adjust our approach without walking away from our calling. Over time, those small, faithful decisions stacked—and they built something sustainable, transferable, and rooted in purpose.

Legacy isn't about perfection.
It's about alignment.
It's about choosing growth *here*—in this season, with what you've been given.

Because your legacy doesn't start someday.
Your legacy starts now.

Your Marriage Mission Statement anchors everything you've learned. It reminds you of:

- Who you are
- Who you are becoming
- What kind of impact your partnership is meant to have

Championships fade.
Statistics get archived.
Titles expire.

Legacy lasts.

And when your marriage is built with intention, conditioned with wisdom, and led with purpose—you don't just win seasons.

You build something that endures.

Championship playing.
Championship living.
Performance-driven partnership.

Closing Thought: Built for More Than the Moment

The most powerful teams—and the strongest marriages—aren't sustained by love alone. They're sustained by mission.

Love may bring two people together, but purpose is what keeps them aligned when the pressure hits, the seasons change, and the applause fades. Purpose gives context to conflict. Direction to decisions. Meaning to sacrifice. It's the difference between reacting in the moment and responding with intention.

Performance, in the context of marriage, isn't about perfection or public wins—it's about *intentional preparation*. It's the daily, often unseen work each spouse commits to so the partnership doesn't just survive but strengthens over time. Performance is choosing self-awareness over avoidance, growth over comfort, and discipline over impulse. It's showing up emotionally present, spiritually grounded, and mentally conditioned—especially when it would be easier to coast. In a true *Performance Partnership*, both spouses understand that legacy isn't built in highlight moments but in consistent effort: how you communicate under stress, how you repair after conflict, how you support one another through transitions, and how you model healthy love for the family watching. That kind of performance creates endurance. And endurance—practiced over time—is what turns a marriage into a legacy that outlives the moment.

That's why your Marriage Mission Statement isn't a formality or a feel-good exercise—it's your playbook for legacy.

It's the anchor you return to when life speeds up.
The standard you measure decisions against.
The reminder—on good days and hard ones—that your
union was never random.

Your marriage was recruited by God, refined by grace, and positioned for impact.

But insight alone doesn't change outcomes.
Execution does.

If you're ready to move from awareness to application—
from good intentions to championship habits—
from surviving seasons to leading with purpose—

Now is the time.

Register today for *Performance Partnership Coaching*™—our elite, confidential, concierge coaching experience designed for professional athletes and high-capacity couples who understand that the long game matters.

This is where clarity becomes strategy.
Where emotional intelligence becomes muscle memory.
Where your marriage stops reacting to pressure and
starts setting the tone.

Don't wait for another season to pass.
Build the partnership your future requires—starting now.

Resource Page

p.6 - MGM Law Firm, "*Common Issues That Arise in Divorce for Professional Athletes*," January 2024, https://www.mgmlawfirm.com/blog/2024/01/common-issues-that-arise-in-divorce-for-professional-athletes/ 1

P 26- https://www.coachhub.com/blog/emotional-intelligence-and-leadership-the-winning-duo-for-companies?utm_source=chatgpt.com 2

p.58-

p.65- Girme, Y. U., N. C. Overall, H. Faingataa, C. G. Sibley, and J. P. L. Tan. "*Emotion Regulation and Relationship Outcomes: The Role of Empathic Accuracy and Partner-Responsive Suppression.*" *Journal of Personality and Social Psychology* 121, no. 6 (2021): 1400–1426.3

p.7- Feinberg, M. E., & Kan, M. L., *Establishing Family Foundations: Effects of a Transition to Parenthood Program on Positive Couples' Skills and Marital Quality*, Journal of Family Psychology 22, no. 6 (2008): 815–825.4

p.83- Gene Upshaw, quoted in "*Emotional Intelligence Helps NFL Players 'Win at Life',*" JM Freedman blog post, July 7, 2008, JM Freedman, "Emotional Intelligence Helps NFL Players 'Win at Life'," accessed [date], https://jmfreedman.com/2008/07/emotional-intelligence-helps-nfl-players-win-at-life/ 5

p.83-84- Miao, Chao, Ronald H. Humphrey, and Shanshan Qian. "A Meta-Analysis of Emotional Intelligence and Work Attitudes." *Journal of Occupational and Organizational Psychology* 90, no. 2 (2017): 177–202.6

p.84- Laborde, Sylvain, Fabrice Dosseville, and Mark S. Allen. "Emotional Intelligence in Sport and Exercise: A Systematic Review." BMC Sports Science, Medicine and Rehabilitation 10, no. 1 (2018).7

p.84- Laborde, S., Dosseville, F., & Allen, M. S. (2018). Emotional intelligence in sport and exercise: A systematic review. BMC Sports Science, Medicine and Rehabilitation, 10(1), Article 1.8

www.ingramcontent.com/pod-product-compliance
Lightning Source LLC
Chambersburg PA
CBHW060348090426
42734CB00011B/2074